Connecticut
WATERFALLS

Chapman Falls is east Connecticut's most celebrated waterfall

Connecticut
WATERFALLS

A GUIDE

Russell Dunn
and
Christy Butler

THE COUNTRYMAN PRESS
WOODSTOCK, VERMONT

If you believe that any information in this guide is incorrect, please let the authors and publisher know so that corrections may be made in future editions. The authors also welcome your comments and suggestions. Address all correspondence to:

>Editor
>*Connecticut Waterfalls*
>The Countryman Press
>PO Box 748
>Woodstock, VT 05091

Many outdoor activities are by their very nature potentially hazardous. The publishers and authors have done their best to ensure the accuracy of all the information in *Connecticut Waterfalls*, however, they can accept no responsibility for any loss, injury, or inconvenience sustained by any traveler as a result of information or advice contained in this guide. **Also, every effort was made to respect private property. Users of *Connecticut Waterfalls* are expected to respect notices of private property.** Future editions of this guide will reflect any changes in land ownership. If you believe any property-related information here to be incorrect, please let us know.

Connecticut Waterfalls

ISBN 978-1-58157-176-9

Book design by Deborah Fillion
Route maps by Erin Greb Cartography, © The Countryman Press
GPS hike maps used by permission, © 2013 Garmin LTD. or its Subsidiaries. All Rights Reserved.
Book composition by PerfecType, Nashville, TN

Published by The Countryman Press
P.O. Box 748, Woodstock, VT 05091

Distributed by W.W. Norton & Company, Inc.
500 Fifth Avenue, New York NY 10110

Printed in the United States of America
10 9 8 7 6 5 4 3 2 1

To our wives—Barbara Delaney and Jan Butler,
who were not only there for us,
but there with us.

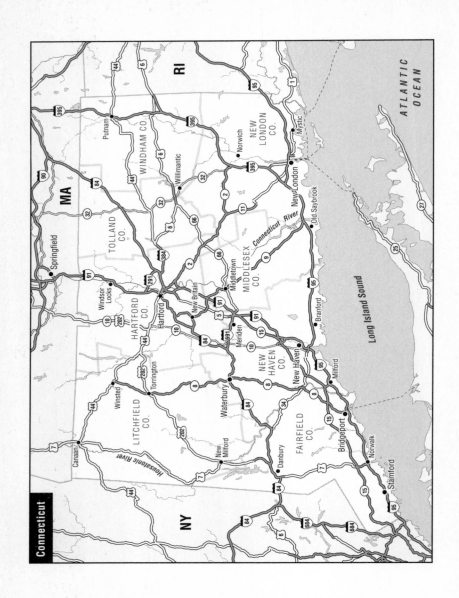

Connecticut

Contents

Aspetuck Falls, New Preston

Acknowledgments

Ardis Abbott, Museum Director, Vernon Historical Society Museum; Carolyn Blouin, Assistant Museum Director, Vernon Historical Society Museum; Dan Bolognani, Executive Director, Upper Housatonic Valley National Heritage Area; Ronald Jones, Chairman of the Upper Housatonic Valley National Heritage Area; David M. Brown, Executive Director, Middlesex Land Trust; William Brown, Director, Eli Whitney Museum; Sally Hill, Associate Director, Eli Whitney Museum; Gregory Davis; Dorothy A. DeBisschop, Oxford Municipal Historian; David Ellis, creator of the Connecticut Waterfalls Website (www.ctwaterfalls.com); the Gilbert Library, particularly Nancy; Diane Hassan, Research Specialist, Danbury Museum and Historical Society; Mike Krenesky, former Municipal Historian of Beacon Falls; John LaShane, founder of the Meshomasic Hiking Club; Mike Maloney, President, Madison Land Conservation Trust, Inc.; Ann Mazeau, Local History Specialist, Burlington Public Library; Mark McEachern, Executive Director, Torrington Historical Society; Greg Miller; Marian O'Keefe, Curator of the Seymour Historical Society; Michael Panus, Department of Energy & Environmental Protection staff; Raymond E. Purtell, Director of Parks and Recreation, Glastonbury; Jackie Shadford, Burlington Historical Society; Deborah Shapiro, Executive Director, Middlesex County Historical Society; Edward M. Smathers; Dave K. Smith, Curator, Manchester Historical Society; Marge Smith, Executive Director, Kent Historical Society; Anne Young, Curator of Library and Archives, Greenwich Historical Society; Allen Weathers, Curator, Meriden Historical Society, Inc.; and Steve Wood.

Special thanks go to our wives, Barbara Delaney and Jan Butler, for their enthusiasm and unfailing patience.

All postcard vimages are from the collection of Russell Dunn.

We are especially grateful to Kermit Hummel, Editorial Director of Countryman Press, and Lisa Sacks, Managing Editor of Countryman Press, for their unfailing help in bringing this book to fruition. Working behind the scenes, they may not get the same degree of recognition that we, as author and photographer, receive, but they are just as deserving.

Nonnewaug Falls, Bethlehem, Litchfield County

Caution & Safety

Readers need to be mindful that they are responsible for themselves once they step into the woods and leave behind the cocoon of civilization. Nature is inherently wild and unpredictable. Unknowable things can happen no matter how well prepared you are—a sprained ankle, a blow delivered by a falling tree limb, getting caught in horrific weather. Trails that were previously unobstructed can suddenly become blocked by blowdown, heavy erosion, or a beaver-created swamp, necessitating some unanticipated changes in plans. The author and publisher can not be held responsible for the vicissitudes of nature, or for any errors, omissions, or inaccuracies that may have crept into this book despite all efforts to the contrary. Nothing can replace common sense and good judgment when it comes to enjoying the great outdoors safely and responsibly.

Crossing rapids hand in hand (postcard)

SAFETY TIPS

1. Stay back from the top of a waterfall regardless of its size. It is easy to be lured out for a closer look, only to suddenly realize how perilous your situation has become as footing gives way and you begin to slide toward the brink.

2. Never dive from or jump off ledges into a pool of water, no matter how inviting it may look. Two things can potentially happen with disastrous and life-changing results: a) You could slip and tumble onto the rocks below, or b) You could collide with an unseen object, like a submerged log or boulder, lurking just below the water's surface.

Just remember—jumping, diving, and climbing around waterfalls can be dangerous. (Multiple exposure shot of boy jumping into Indian Well)

3. Resist the urge to swim in a pool near the top of a cascade. If the current is strong enough and the water sufficiently deep, you could be swept along over the top of the falls, with nothing to grab hold of to stop your forward momentum.

4. Don't throw rocks over the top of a high waterfall to hear them crash or splash below. There's always the possibility that someone unknown to you may have just walked into the trajectory of your throw.

5. Refrain from climbing up waterfalls or surrounding rock walls. Many waterfalls and their surrounding bedrock are formed in sedimentary rock (like shale), which can easily crumble as you reach for safe handholds and footholds. Rocks surrounding waterfalls also tend to be wet from lack of sunlight and, in the case of large falls, from spray sent aloft from falling water. Slippery surfaces make for dangerous footing.

6. Take photos from the bottom of waterfalls whenever possible. By doing so you will be assured of the best views and optimum photo shoots while remaining safe from being lured to the edge of a high precipice.

7. Watch out for ticks, which can cause Lyme disease. Check yourself over thoroughly when you leave the woods.

8. Never drink water from streams. The threat of giardiasis (caused by an intestinal parasite) is simply too real to be ignored.

9. Always hike with two or more companions. Should someone get hurt, then one person can stay with him or her while the other goes for help.

10. Bring along a day pack, complete with cell phone, emergency supplies, compass, whistle, flashlight, dry matches, rain gear, energy bars, extra layers, gorp, duct tape, lots of water (at least 24 ounces per person), mosquito repellent, emergency medical kit, and sunblock. You never know when you might need a particular item unexpectedly.

11. Wear sunblock when outside for extended periods of time and repellents when it is likely you'll be sharing the woods with mosquitoes or black flies. A hat with a wide brim for keeping off the sun can also be helpful. Remember that you can get sunburned even on a cloudy day.

Wearing long pants and a long sleeve shirt also make sense if you want to reduce your exposure to the sun and biting insects. One substitute for repellents is to bring along a "swisher"—a leafy branch that you can wave around to sweep the air free of biting insects.

12. Wear ankle-high boots for support and optimal traction, benefits which your sneakers and shoes can't provide. During winter, bring along stabilizers or crampons in case you encounter ice.

13. Be mindful of hypothermia and stay dry. You don't need to be exposed to near-freezing temperatures to become chilled when wet. Should

you accidentally get drenched in the spring, fall, or winter, return to your car immediately.

The opposite of hypothermia is hyperthermia, caused by the body overheating. To mitigate this problem, drink plenty of water when the weather is hot and muggy, and stay in the shade whenever possible. Should you become hyperthermic, get out of the sun immediately and immerse yourself in cool water if a stream is close at hand.

14. Avoid deep woods during hunting season. If you do venture out, wear bright colors and make periodic, loud noises to draw attention to yourself.

15. Stay on trails whenever possible to avoid becoming lost or disoriented. If you follow a stream up to a waterfall, return the same way.

16. Always tell someone where you are going, when you will return, and what to do if you have not shown up by the designated time.

17. Avoid any creature that is acting erratically, a possible indication that it is either rabid or operating in a predatory mode.

18. Use good judgment, something which can be difficult to exercise under all circumstances. Unless it is critical to respond immediately, stop for a moment and think through what your options are. This is particularly true if you suddenly feel lost or disoriented.

The old football adage "The best defense is a good offense" applies equally as well to hiking. It's far better to defuse a problem early on than to wait until it has reached crisis proportions.

19. Start early in the morning if you are doing a long hike. That way you'll maximize the hours of daylight, creating a greater margin of safety should the hike take longer than expected. Allow more time if you are hiking during the winter, when there are fewer hours of daylight.

Introduction

Think of Connecticut and it is unlikely that waterfalls will come foremost to mind. After all, isn't Connecticut best known for its seaports and its proximity to New York City? Like all preconceptions, however, this one is ready to be challenged, especially now that you are holding this book firmly in hand; for Connecticut is truly a land of tumbling cascades, plunges, and waterslides—and many, by good fortune (not to mention the hard work of dedicated individuals and organizations), are contained in public parks and on state lands.

What kind of waterfalls are we talking about? In the early 1920s Wallace Nutting, author of *Connecticut Beautiful,* wrote that "in Connecticut there are numerous highlands which afford us pleasing, rather than stupendous, waterfalls." Although Wallace may have been the first author of note to sum up the nature of Connecticut's waterfalls, he seriously underestimated their majesty. Connecticut not only is characterized by its pleasing and pastoral waterfalls, it also has some spectacular, first-rate falls—Kent Falls, Campbell Falls, the Great Falls of the Housatonic, Roaring Brook Falls, Chapman Falls, and Buttermilk Falls, just to name several.

To be sure, Connecticut is not a large state compared to most of the others in the United States (in fact, it's the third smallest), but four hundred years of accrued European history, as well as the less recorded oral history of Native Americans, give its landscape a depth of history unraveled by virtually any other state in the country. Geographically, Connecticut is roughly 110 miles in length, going east to west, and 70 miles in width, going north to south, and divided into two uneven halves by the Connecticut River.

Although the Connecticut River is strongly identified with the state of Connecticut, it also passes through New Hampshire, Vermont, and Massachusetts, knitting together much of New England. It truly is a four-state river, full-grown and well fed by numerous tributaries along its way south between the Connecticut Lakes in New Hampshire and the Atlantic Ocean below Connecticut. It is a journey of 407 miles from start to finish.

Besides the Connecticut River, the state's two other prominent waterways are the Thames River in eastern Connecticut (a very short river) and the Housatonic River in western Connecticut.

Sperry Falls near Woodbridge

Connecticut is represented by four main regions of topographic diversity—the Taconic Mountains, the Central Valley, the eastern and western Uplands, and the coastal plains. This book will focus on the Taconic Mountains, the western and eastern Uplands, and the more northern sections of the Central Valley. Generally speaking, the coastal plains in the south are simply too lacking in elevation to produce waterfalls of any note.

Connecticut's waterways are largely a result of the end of the last Ice Age as retreating glaciers sculpted the landscape, leaving behind over a thousand lakes and ponds. The bountiful presence of these bodies of water ensure that a fairly consistent supply of water is maintained for waterfall production.

The name Connecticut has Native American roots, going back to the Algonquian who called the river *kwenihtekot,* meaning "long tidal river." From this simple beginning first arose the name of the river; then the colony; then finally the state.

The first white man to explore the Connecticut River was Adriaen Block, who sailed up it in 1614 in a 44-foot-long boat. Block Island, near the entrance to Long Island Sound, is named after him. Block called the river *versh,* meaning the "freshwater river." Block was also the first white man to explore the Housatonic River.

Native Americans were the first people in Connecticut to gaze upon waterfalls with wonderment and awe. In all likelihood they believed that the myriad of cascades encountered, seemingly pouring out of the skies, were created by the Great Spirit—an unseen mystical entity who dwelled high above in the mountains where the lifeblood of streams originated.

Native Americans might have made use of waterfalls for special occasions—the inauguration of a new chief, the celebration of a marriage, the rites of passage of a young hunter into manhood—or perhaps they were sought out by shamans and tribal leaders on vision quests. Surely waterfalls were perceived as powerful centers of spirituality.

With the arrival of Europeans in the early 1600s, however, the perception of waterfalls changed profoundly. Initially explorers and settlers may have found waterfalls and rapids on large rivers like the Connecticut, Housatonic, Farmington, Quinebaug, and Shetucket to be nuisances, for these natural barriers effectively blocked the passage of large ships carrying passengers and cargo inland, causing the outward migration of settlers entering the New World from Europe to slow down to a crawl.

It didn't take long, however, for this initial perception to change to one of gratitude and appreciation. Within a matter of decades Dutch and English settlers were exploiting the power of waterfalls to liberate them from the oppressive drudgeries of daily life, for the world in which they lived was one with limited energy alternatives. At best the available sources were manpower, domesticated animals, wind, and water. Humans, to be sure, were able to do comparatively little work. Domesticated animals, principally oxen and horses, while powerful, could sicken, die, or become petulant and unruly, and certainly demanded time and energy for their upkeep. And while wind was free and available, it was inconsistent and best relied upon near coastal regions or high atop mountain summits—places where industries were not likely to flourish. Waterfalls and fast-moving streams, however, provided renewable, abundant, reliable, and clean sources of energy (the latter a fact not fully appreciated in those early days). Industrialists in droves turned to waterfalls to drive massive overshot waterwheels which converted the power of tumbling water into mechanical energy to drive grinders, presses, bellows, vertical saws, buzz saws, and more elaborate machinery as time went on. Waterwheels could do the work of many animals without any of the inconveniences.

If you read the 19th century literature, it becomes readily apparent that industrialists considered streams wasteful and inefficient if their waterpower couldn't be "improved" upon. At issue here was not only the lack of enough waterfalls to go around, but a lack of enough streams with adequate water flow. The creation of artificial waterfalls—dams—solved this problem, and dams grew in numbers exponentially. Thanks to dams impounding millponds, numerous factories were able to proliferate on non-waterfall-bearing streams.

By the 19th century, waterfalls (artificial and natural) had become the driving force behind the Industrial Revolution in the eastern United States, and this was certainly true in Connecticut, particularly its northern regions. Undoubtedly waterfalls would have continued to serve in this capacity for an indefinite time were it not for two major events which occurred virtually simultaneously starting in the mid-to-late 1800s. First, the forests that had initially seemed inexhaustible were quickly consumed by timber-hungry mills and factories. Conservation was still a concept in its infancy. Once the trees were gone, there was no more hemlock bark for the tanneries; no more wood to produce charcoal to satisfy the high-temperature requirements of kilns; no more lumber for making furniture and building houses; no more ash to make potash; no more logs to heat homes; and no tall white pines to produce tall ships' masts. The industries had simply exploited to virtual extinction the materials upon which their factories depended.

Secondly, fossil fuels were discovered—oil, natural gas, and particularly coal, which the United States possessed in enormous quantities. Fossil fuels provided mill and factory operators with a degree of mobility that was previously unattainable. Industrialists were no longer physically bound to waterfalls and could now move closer to rivers for easier transport of goods, or closer to areas where natural resources could be mined or manipulated with increased efficiency, or closer to centers of population where workers could be hired without a great deal of effort. Thus a good number of factories and mills situated next to waterfalls were abandoned in favor of other sites that didn't depend upon waterpower.

The age of electricity soon arrived, replacing hydropower with hydroelectric power. Appleton, Wisconsin, constructed the first modern hydroelectric dam in 1882. In virtually no time at all, hundreds of hydroelectric plants were flourishing, and by the beginning of the 20th century, over 60 percent of the energy produced was hydroelectric power. Ironically, although hydroelectric plants were quickly adopted in Europe, the Europeans put many of them underground (thus preserving the natural beauty of the waterfall), whereas in the United States the decision was made to build above ground, partly to save money. Perhaps also the exposed plants were thought to be good public relations for the country, symbolizing the United States' power and domination over nature, just as belching smokestacks came to symbolize the advent of the Industrial Revolution.

Today many waterfalls have returned to a preindustrial state, no longer bound by industrialists to waterwheels and turbines. Connecticut, wisely, has made an effort to preserve its natural wonders, and many waterfalls now form the centerpieces of its parks and preserves. Without the efforts of many in preserving the best of Connecticut, a book of Connecticut waterfalls would have been impossible.

WHAT IS A WATERFALL?

The most ready answer that comes to mind is "what looks like a waterfall is a waterfall"—a statement that, though simplistic, reflects the subjectivity of one's own aesthetic experiences. Even the world's most prominent waterfall experts would be hard-pressed to agree on when falling waters are a waterfall, and when they are simply just falling waters. Some might insist, for instance, that only waterfalls higher than 6 feet (or any arbitrary number) are true waterfalls. Others might argue that cascades have to be significantly inclined, say to at least a 70-degree angle, before they can be considered waterfalls rather than just cascading streams. Still others might contend that waterfalls have to "fall" in order to be *true* waterfalls, readily dismissing those that remain in constant contact with the bedrock—and yet there are many beautiful waterfalls in this book that fly in the face of each one of these arbitrary definitions.

What counts in the end is what appeals to you. When it comes to waterfalls, ultimately you are your own authority.

WATERFALLS ARE FOR EVERYONE

Every effort has been made to ensure that at least one or two waterfalls are represented for every level of hiking ability. Some waterfalls, for instance, require more effort to reach due to their higher elevation or greater distance from the trailhead. They will appeal to readers who enjoy a vigorous hike. Roaring Brook Falls and Spruce Glen Falls represent waterfall hikes of this type.

Other waterfalls can be seen from a car window or from a short, level walk to an overlook. These are roadside waterfalls that don't require any substantial effort to reach. They will appeal to elderly waterfall lovers or those with disabilities. The lower half of Kent Falls (visible from the parking lot), Tartia Falls near Middle Hampton, and Buttermilk Falls at Norfolk are excellent examples of these kinds of waterfalls.

To be sure, most of the waterfalls presented fall in between these two categories. Waterfalls come in endless varieties of shapes and sizes, with no two ever being exactly identical appearance-wise. Some are steeply cascading streams that race wildly downhill, never losing contact with the underlying bedrock; others plunge off cliff edges and remain airborne until they crash below. Many, if not most, are a combination of the two. Some waterfalls drop only once, while many others come bouncing down step by step, as though on a giant staircase. Some waterfalls splash onto rock slabs and boulders that have accumulated at their base, while others plunge into pools of water.

Even the same waterfall never looks exactly the same from one day or month to the next. Erosive processes cause sections of waterfalls or side walls to periodically break off; boulders and massive tree trunks are occasionally forced over the top of falls by sudden deluges, gathering below or farther downstream in tangled jumbles; and trees along the side walls inevitably lose their purchase and tumble into the gorge. All of these phenomena alter the way the waterfall and the surrounding landscape look.

What's more, each waterfall goes through seasonal changes. In spring they are blurs of undulating white as streams overflow with snowmelt. In summer they become increasingly rocklike as water levels recede and more of the surrounding bedrock is exposed. In fall they are transfixing with the

Low-water view of the Great Falls of the Housatonic River from the east side

awesome colors of autumn. And in winter, waterfalls hibernate until summoned again by spring's warmth.

Gaze into the falling waters and you will see eternity passing before your eyes; patterns endlessly changing but never repeating as molecules of water vanish downstream, not to reappear for millenniums until precipitation brings them back inland from the ocean.

BEST TIME TO VISIT

There are trade-offs no matter what time you go waterfalling. Without question, waterfalls put on their most dynamic show during the springtime. The big waterfalls literally shake the ground with their might, roaring and bellowing as they try to disgorge impossible amounts of water from overflowing streams. Because the forest is leafless in early spring, the lack of foliage virtually gives you X-ray vision as you peer through skeletal woods at waterfalls that later in the season are obscured from view. And if you're out before black fly season begins, the air is relatively free of biting insects. The downside is that if too much water is flowing, many of the interesting surface features of the waterfall (such as ledges, potholes, and overhangs) are lost. Furthermore, the lack of tree cover often gives photographs taken a rather gray and lackluster quality.

Summer has much to offer for waterfall enthusiasts. The temperature is generally pleasant, the forest is green and bustling with life, and waterfalls (now less engorged by water) reveal interesting rock features. If you're hot, you can cool off in the stream or you can simply rest along the bank. The only downside is the inevitable biting insects and the possibility that the flow of water has been reduced so much that little water is coming over the waterfall.

In some ways autumn may be the closest thing to an ideal time to go waterfalling. Trees are no longer sucking up billions of gallons of water to produce wood, which means that streams have been reanimated and waterfalls have become more fully developed, but not so engorged as to hide many of their interesting rock features. The colors of fall are brilliant and make for wonderful picture-taking and, in late fall, biting insects are virtually gone until next year. The downside to autumn is that you may have to share the waterfall with many other hikers and photographers who have ventured out for the same reasons that enticed you.

As far as winter goes, there is a quiet beauty to behold, but in most instances the waterfall has turned into a wall of ice or an inverted ice cone, creating a fairly inanimate subject for waterfall appreciation. Although there are no biting insects to annoy you, the coldness can be a disincentive, particularly at waterfall sites where the deep snow and ice make it colder than the surrounding woods.

HOW BEST TO VIEW WATERFALLS

We strongly recommend that you do your viewing and picture-taking from the bottom of waterfalls whenever possible. This will increase your safety tenfold. Many waterfall-related deaths occur while hikers are moving about at the top of large waterfalls. Enthusiasts get too close to the brink, lose their footing, and are swept over—something which can happen literally in the blink of an eye. Many hikers fail to realize that the streambed at the top of a waterfall can be wet and slimy, and therefore slippery; it can also slope just enough so that you begin to slide forward with nothing to grab hold of like an insect drawn into a pitcher plant.

Stand at the bottom and look up. Not only will you get the best pictures from this vantage point, but you'll be back to take more another day.

WATERFALLS AS ART

In 2008 Berlin-based artist Olafur Eliasson created a waterfall spectacle for New York City entitled *New York City Waterfalls*. The exhibit consisted of artificially created waterfalls erected at four different locations on the Hudson River—beneath the Brooklyn Bridge, between piers 4 and 5 in Brooklyn, at lower Manhattan at pier 35 (north of Rutgers Street), and on the north shore of Governors Island.

The waterfalls were ingenuously created by erecting scaffolding near the edge of the waterfront. From the top of this structure, 35,000 gallons of water were then released each minute to form a continuous sheet of falling water. Each waterfall stood between 90 and 120 feet high, making them, as far as waterfalls go, respectable in size. No doubt in the future, new, even-larger artificial waterfalls will be created for artistic purposes.

More recently, the new 9/11 Memorial in New York City was unveiled with its centerpiece being—what else—waterfalls.

It should come as no surprise then that Connecticut also has its artificial waterfalls. Mohegan Sun casino in Uncasville features perhaps the most striking one. A 55-foot-high artificial waterfall provides diners with a relaxing background ambiance—a superb melding of the natural and artificial.

Over the years photographers have taken breathtaking pictures of Connecticut's waterfalls as they gaze through the camera lens with the eye of an

The riverbed at Bulls Bridge, littered with potholes of all sizes

artist. Their names and Websites can be found in the Additional Resources section near the end of the book.

THE PHYSICALITY OF WATERFALLS

Waterfalls are energetic agents of destruction, literally dismantling mountains and hillsides one pebble, stone, and boulder at a time. Their assault is so relentless that each waterfall will eventually destroy even itself. Niagara Falls serves a ready example of what is yet to come. Over the last ten thousand years the waterfall has worked its way 7 miles up the Niagara River, steadily gaining elevation while carving out a deep gorge. When Niagara Falls finally reaches Lake Erie, it will cease to exist, a victim of its own onslaught. So it is with all waterfalls when looked at over enormous intervals of time.

But waterfalls do more than just break apart the surrounding bedrock. They also break apart sunlight. The larger, more powerful waterfalls do it by sending up a plume of spray which, in turn, bends sunlight through millions of water-drop prisms, turning the saturated air into a rainbow.

Waterfalls' physicality even extends to sound. Listen closely the next time you visit a waterfall. Vary your position relative to the top and bottom of the waterfall and two distinct sounds may emerge, the first being the sound of the stream going over the top of the waterfall (producing a white-noise "hiss") and the second, the sound produced as the water arrives at the bottom, crashing onto rocks or splashing into a plunge pool. Sound, of course, also varies according to season. The thunderous waterfall that deafened you in the early spring is often a quiet trickle in the summer.

GETTING THERE

It doesn't matter if a guidebook has prize-winning pictures or a Nobel laureate narrative. If the book fails to get you to the trailhead, then everything else becomes academic. For this reason particular emphasis has been made on providing directions that are clear and concise, starting from easily located road intersections close to cities and villages.

In addition, *Delorme Connecticut/Rhode Island Atlas and Gazetteer* coordinates and GPS coordinates have been included in the header for each chapter. The *Delorme Atlas and Gazetteer* coordinates give you the big picture, delineating the general area around the trailhead, including nearby roads. The GPS coordinates supply the little picture, narrowing down the location of the trailhead parking area to a pinpoint. Each provides what the other lacks.

Taken together—the written directions, the *Delorme Connecticut/Rhode Island Atlas and Gazetteer* quadrants, and GPS coordinates—readers should find the experience of getting to the trailhead reasonably straightforward and free of frustration.

DEGREE OF DIFFICULTY

It's impossible not to be subjective when rating the "degree of difficulty" that each hike presents, for the obvious reason that individuals vary greatly in terms of ability, age, and conditioning. These factors, furthermore, are affected by the season and vicissitudes of weather. No one feels quite as peppy, for instance, when the temperature is a muggy 95 degrees.

Presumably the average 90-year-old will have more difficulty negotiating an "easy" 0.2-mile trek than the average 25-year-old; a super-fit triathlete probably won't even break into a sweat climbing up a steep ravine, while a couch potato will be winded within 100 feet. Alas, what is easy for one may be difficult for another. For this reason keep in mind that general guidelines are helpful only when applied to the "average" hiker. Taking this into account, the following categories have been put together to provide crude guidelines:

Easy—short distance, generally less than 0.5 mile; no real effort required to complete the hike.

Moderately easy—short distance, but with some effort required; or, less than 1.0 mile over flat, nontaxing terrain.

Moderate—less than 1.0 mile trek over mixed terrain; some effort required.

Moderately difficult—less than 1.5-mile hike over mixed terrain; or, less than 1.0 mile, but involving an appreciable ascent with more effort required.

Difficult—greater than 1.0-mile trek with appreciable ascent and increasing effort required; or, greater than 2.0 miles with some effort needed

Very difficult—regardless of distance, the hike requires maximum effort due to steep ascents and/or difficult terrain being encountered.

Hiking mileages given are one-way unless otherwise stated.

Litchfield County: Dean's Ravine Falls, North of West Cornwall, Mohawk Trail

Connecticut Counties Covered in This Book

LITCHFIELD COUNTY is named after Lichfield, the cathedral city of Staffordshire, England. The *t* was added at a later date for apparently unknown reasons. The county of rolling hills and deep valleys, organized in 1752, is tucked into the expansive northwest corner of Connecticut. Litchfield is the largest county in the state and covers a total of 945 square miles, 920 square miles of which is on land and 25 square miles on water. In addition it contains the Litchfield Hills (the Berkshire section of the Appalachian Mountains) as well as a number of high peaks, culminating at 2,380 feet on the mountainside of Mt. Frissel, virtually on the border between Massachusetts and Connecticut.

FAIRFIELD COUNTY is located in the southwestern part of Connecticut, delineated by Litchfield County and the Housatonic River to the north; Litchfield County, New Haven County, and the Housatonic River to the east; New York State to the west; and the Long Island Sound to the south. Parts of both the Taconic Mountains and Berkshire Mountains run through this county. The county's highest elevation is 1,290 feet, south of Branch Hill on the border with New York State. Fairfield County encompasses 620 square miles of land and 211 square miles of water. The southern part of the county is called the Gold Coast because of its accumulated wealth, accrued by many of its residents who commute to New York City.

HARTFORD COUNTY contains 735 square miles of land, 15 square miles of water, and is bisected by the Connecticut River. It was one of the four original Connecticut counties to be established in 1666 by the Connecticut General Court. The county, which occupies the north-central part of the state, is named after the city of Hartford, founded in 1635. Originally the city was called Newtown but the name was changed to Hartford in 1637 to honor the English town of Hertford.

The Connecticut River, which passes by the city of Hartford, is a large and powerful river, and one that can not be treated cavalierly. All too often settlers have underestimated its ferocity and established homes and villages

The rarely seen upper cascade at Tartia Falls

too close to its banks. This was particularly true for the city of Hartford in April of 1909 when the Connecticut River reached a (then) record-breaking flood stage of 24.5 feet above the low-water mark. The city flooded, with a considerable loss of property as a result. Hurricane Irene in 2011 posed similar problems for the Connecticut River valley.

NEW HAVEN COUNTY is located in the south-central part of Connecticut and encompasses a total area of 862 square miles, 606 square miles of which is land and 256 square miles water. New Haven is one of the four original counties in Connecticut. The other three are New London, Fairfield, and Hartford. Near the coast and along the Housatonic River the terrain is mostly flat, rising up as you head northward to a high point of 1,050 feet above sea level in the town of Wolcott. The county's most notable geographic landmarks are Sleeping Giant, and West Rock and East Rock. New Haven was originally called Quinnipiac after a Native American tribe.

MIDDLESEX COUNTY consists of 369 square miles of land and 70 square miles of water. Located in the south-central part of Connecticut, it was stitched together in 1785 from portions of Hartford and New London. Its highest point, located in Meshomasic State Forest, is 916 feet above sea level. The county is relatively flat, rising gently uphill from the Atlantic Ocean and the Connecticut River valley.

TOLLAND COUNTY is located in the north-central section of Connecticut. It is the smallest county in the state, containing 410 square miles, 7 square miles of it being water. The county formed in 1785 from towns in Windham County.

WINDHAM COUNTY occupies the northeastern portion of the state, created in 1726 from pieces taken from Harford and New London Counties. It covers 521 square miles, of which 9 square miles is water. The county is informally called the Quiet Corner, for its landscape is more bucolic and serene than the hustle and bustle common in sections of the southern part of the state. Still, its tranquility is deceptive; in years past, its streams and rivers powered numerous textile mills.

NEW LONDON COUNTY is located in the southeast corner of the state and was established in 1666, one of the original four counties in Connecticut. Its terrain is mostly level, the highest point being Gates Hill (660 feet). The county covers 772 square miles, of which 106 square miles are water.

Campbell Falls, Northwest of Norfolk

Part I: Western Connecticut

There are five counties covered in this section:

Litchfield County
Fairfield County
Hartford County
New Haven County
Middlesex County

For more information on each county, see page XXIX.

FALLS ACCESSIBLE FROM US 7

US 7 enters Connecticut from Ashley Falls, Massachusetts, and quickly heads south, passing through Canaan, a medium-sized village bordered by picturesque hills and contained within the Blackberry River and Housatonic River valley systems. Paralleling it are CT 41 to the west and CT 272 to the east. Both lead past areas that are of interest to waterfallers.

Once US 7 reaches Falls Village (roughly 6.5 miles south of the Connecticut border), it falls into lockstep with the Housatonic River until it reaches the hamlet of Still River. Here US 7 switches loyalties to the Still River and follows it to West Danbury, an area known for the manufacturing of hats. At this point, US 7 takes off on its own until it picks up the Norwalk River northwest of Topstone. Proceeding onward, US 7 then follows the Norwalk River all the way downstate to I-95 in Norwalk, just upriver from Norwalk Harbor at the Atlantic Ocean.

The journey on US 7 is a longitudinal (vertical) one. The other relevant routes leading off latitudinally are US 44 east to Norfolk and west to Salisbury, CT 341 east to East Kent and west to Macedonia, and CT 15 east toward Weston and west toward New Canaan.

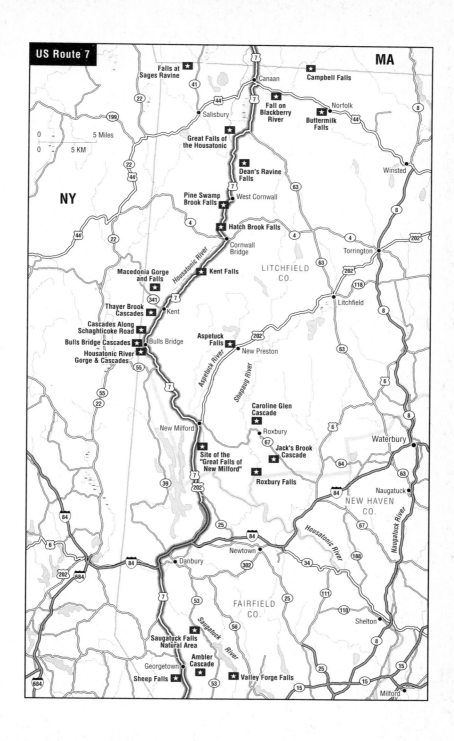

US Route 7

MA

NY

Falls at
Sages Ravine ★

Campbell Falls ★

Canaan

41

44

Fall on
Blackberry
River ★

Norfolk

8

Salisbury

Buttermilk
Falls ★

44

22

199

0   5 Miles

0   5 KM

22

44

Great Falls of
the Housatonic ★

Dean's Ravine
Falls ★

Winsted

Pine Swamp
Brook Falls ★

West Cornwall

63

Hatch Brook Falls ★

4

8

4

4

202

Cornwall
Bridge

Torrington

Housatonic River

LITCHFIELD
CO.

63

202

Macedonia Gorge
and Falls ★

Kent Falls ★

118

341

Litchfield

8

Thayer Brook
Cascades ★

Kent

7

Cascades Along
Schaghticoke Road ★

Aspetuck
Falls ★

202

63

Bulls Bridge Cascades ★

Bulls Bridge

New Preston

6

Housatonic River
Gorge & Cascades ★

55

Aspetuck River

Shepaug River

55

22

7

Caroline Glen
Cascade ★

8

New Milford

Roxbury

Waterbury

67

Jack's Brook
Cascade ★

Site of the
"Great Falls of
New Milford" ★

64

63

7

39

202

Roxbury Falls ★

84

Naugatuck

NEW HAVEN
CO.

84

67

Naugatuck River

Housatonic River

188

25

84

6

Newtown

Danbury

302

34

111

202

684

7

53

25

110

Shelton

FAIRFIELD
CO.

58

Saugatuck River

8

Saugatuck Falls
Natural Area ★

Ambler
Cascade ★

25

15

684

Georgetown

Sheep Falls ★

53

Valley Forge Falls ★

15

15

Milford

CAMPBELL FALLS

Location: Northwest of Norfolk (on the border between Massachusetts and Connecticut), Campbell Falls State Park
Delorme Connecticut/Rhode Island Atlas and Gazetteer: p. 50, A7; **Estimated GPS:** 41°02.70'N; 73°13.91'W
Views: Head-on
Aesthetics: Excellent

Characteristics: Remote, scenic, robust, large
Accessibility: 0.2-mile walk down a fairly graded trail to base of falls
Degree of Difficulty: Moderately easy
Information: Trail map available at http://www.ct.gov/dep/lib/dep /stateparks/maps/campbellfalls.pdf

DESCRIPTION: Campbell Falls is a dramatic, two-tier waterfall on the Whiting River—a medium-sized stream which rises from Thousand Acres Swamp and East Indies Pond and flows into the Blackberry River east of East Canaan. The stream races down through a narrow cleft in granitic gneiss bedrock, dropping more than 60 feet in two giant steps—with the upper drop being the larger of the two.

Immediately upstream, just above the falls, the Whiting River flows under an old stone bridge, from where several small cascades can be seen.

HISTORY: Campbell Falls is at Campbell Falls State Park—a fairly remote, 102-acre preserve whose waterfall is most assuredly the park's main attraction and centerpiece. The White Memorial Foundation of Litchfield, Connecticut, gave Campbell Falls State Park to the State of Connecticut and the Commonwealth of Massachusetts; in 1923 both states placed the park under permanent protection. Concrete columns mark the boundary line delineating Connecticut from Massachusetts.

Campbell Falls is one of 139 state parks that have been created in Connecticut since 1913.

During pre–Revolutionary War days, John Campbell operated a gristmill at the falls. It is his name that has become attached to the waterfall.

Later the falling waters of the Whiting River powered a sawmill.

DIRECTIONS: From Norfolk (junction of US 44 and CT 272), drive north on CT 272 (North Street) for 4.2 miles. Turn left onto Campbell Falls Road, drive west for 0.4 mile, and then turn left into a parking area.

Campbell Falls on the border between Connecticut and Massachusetts

From the parking lot walk downhill for less than 0.2 mile and then bear right to reach the base of Campbell Falls for unobstructed views.

To reach the smaller, upper cascades, walk west from the parking area along Campbell Falls Road for several hundred feet until you arrive at the stone bridge that spans the Whiting River. Tiny cascades are visible upstream from the bridge.

Cross over the bridge and then immediately follow a tiny path to your left that leads down 30 feet to views atop Campbell Falls. Go no further. Just up ahead is the top of Campbell Falls where an unwary hiker could lose footing and be swept over the brink.

Turn around and look upstream. More cascades, not initially evident, can be seen beneath the stone bridge.

2

BUTTERMILK FALLS

Location: Norfolk (Litchfield County)

Delorme Connecticut/Rhode Island Atlas and Gazetteer: p. 50, D9; **Estimated GPS:** Site #1—41°59.67'N; 73°12.14'W; Site #2—41°59.45'N; 73°12.28'W

Views: Site #1—Head-on, distant; Site #2—Head-on, lateral

Aesthetics: Good

Characteristics: Urban, historic, medium-sized

Accessibility: Site #1—Roadside or 75-foot walk downhill to river for a closer view; Site #2—Lateral views from top of bank, 30-foot descent to base of falls

Degree of Difficulty: Easy to moderately easy

DESCRIPTION: Buttermilk Falls is a 20-foot-high cascade on the Blackberry River—a medium-sized stream which rises south of Norfolk and flows into the Housatonic River west of Canaan. The river, upon entering the village, spills over an old mill dam, passes under a tiny bridge, and then cascades down a steep rock face, fanning out to form Buttermilk Falls.

Several hundred yards downriver from the base of Buttermilk Falls, a tiny tributary called Wood Creek flows into the Blackberry River. In doing so it produces several small cascades, finally dropping over a 2-foot-high block at the confluence of the two streams.

HISTORY: Buttermilk Falls is a fairly generic name for a waterfall, analogous to Bald Mountain for a treeless peak. There are two principal Buttermilk Falls in Connecticut, and both are located within Litchfield County. The second waterfall is near Hancock, southeast of Plymouth (see the chapter in Falls Accessible from CT 8, Buttermilk Falls [Tolles]).

A grist mill and blacksmith shop once operated at the top of the falls. Using hydropower furnished by the Blackberry River, mills along the river produced a variety of items, including linseed oil, men's hats, cheese boxes, woolens, scythes, and hoes.

Norfolk is named for the English county of Norfolk, known as the "icebox of Connecticut" due to its often harsh winters. It is an area where only dairy farming is agriculturally feasible.

DIRECTIONS: From Canaan (junction of US 7 and US 44) drive east on US 44 (Norfolk Road) for 7.0 miles to Norfolk (junction of US 44 and CT 272).

The centerpiece of Norfolk—Buttermilk Falls

Site #1: Park next to the World War I memorial located in a park at the center of a tiny, triangular intersection. From the memorial green, walk south across US 44 over to a tiny park which leads down a grassy knoll to the Blackberry River in 75 feet. There are excellent views of Buttermilk Falls from the road or from the bottom of the hill by the Blackberry River.

A well-maintained informal path leads from the bottom of the hill along the east bank to near the base of the falls, a distance of several hundred feet.

Just downriver from the southwest corner of the park is Wood Creek. A 2-foot-high cascade can be seen at its confluence with the Blackberry River.

Site #2: From the memorial green, drive south on CT 272 for a hundred feet. Turn right onto Westside Road and head uphill for several hundred feet. Just before you cross over a tiny bridge spanning the Blackberry River, look for a plaque to the right that reads THIS SITE IS GIVEN TO THE TOWN OF NORFOLK BY MRS. OLIVIA JACOBSON. OCT. 15, 1963. Pull over here. This tiny tract of land consists of a pretty garden delineated by a walk-around, and a stone flight of stairs that leads down to near the base of the falls. A conveniently placed bench provides for rest and contemplation.

3

WATERFALL ON BLACKBERRY RIVER

Location: East Canaan (Litchfield County)
Delorme Connecticut/Rhode Island Atlas and Gazetteer: p. 50, C4; **Estimated GPS:** 41°00.65'N; 73°17.58'W
Views: Head-on

Aesthetics: Fair
Characteristics: Remote, historic, partially dammed
Accessibility: Roadside, 100-foot walk for close-up view
Degree of Difficulty: Easy

DESCRIPTION: This small cascade is at the south end of a 12-foot-high dam on the Blackberry River—a medium-sized stream which rises south of Norfolk and flows into the Housatonic River west of Canaan.

At one time a substantial cascade existed here, but the present dam integrated most of it, leaving only a small fraction still exposed. Evidence of this former cascade remains, however. Look closely and you will see that the streambed above the dam is 10 feet higher than below it.

Up until the early 20th century the penstock (the large pipe that you see emerging from the dam) carried water to the turbine, which turned a large crown gear. The gear, in turn, drove a blowing engine, which created an airflow brought down to a preheating oven on the side of the furnace—and finally, once heated, into the furnace stack itself.

The Beckley Blast Furnace gives you the rare opportunity to see how waterfalls and dams were harnessed to do actual work during the 19th and 20th centuries. In most instances waterfalls powered overshot waterwheels. In the case of the Beckley Blast Furnace site, a turbine utilized the power of moving water.

HISTORY: As on-site historical markers erected by the Friends of Beckley Furnace point out, you are visiting an area whose history is one of heavy industrialization. The first Catalan forge was built here in 1739. Samuel Forbes and his brother, Elisha, established a new forge in 1759.

In 1847 John Adam Beckley built the Beckley Blast Furnace (the one visible today) to smelt pig iron—a crude form of iron which can be refined to produce steel or wrought iron. The furnace was primarily made out of

The Blackberry River, at one time a major source of waterpower

The Beckley Blast Furnace (ca. 1960 postcard)

marble quarried locally. At the end of World War I in 1919 the furnace shut down due to the dwindling demand for iron.

In 1978, the Beckley Blast Furnace was placed on the National Register of Historic Places and in 1999 the stack was stabilized and restored to its present condition. Originally the furnace stack, with its 30-by-30-foot square base, rose up to a height of 32 feet. After a fire nearly destroyed the furnace in 1880, the stack was rebuilt in 1896 and an additional 8 feet of chimney was added on, transforming the stack into one of the tallest in the area.

Multiple historical plaques and a kiosk next to the furnace and dam, including illustrations and photographs, recount the history of the site. Old rusted artifacts lay scattered about, allowing you the rare opportunity to put the pieces together in your own mind to imagine how the past once looked.

DIRECTIONS: From Canaan (junction of US 7 and US 44) proceed east on US 44 (Norfolk Road) for 2.3 miles, and then turn right onto Lower Road.

From Norfolk (junction of US 44 and CT 272), drive west on US 44 for 4.6 miles, and then turn left onto Lower Road.

Approaching from either direction, follow Lower Road south, going gradually downhill, for 0.5 mile. Then turn left onto a small dirt road that leads immediately down to the Blackberry River. Park next to the Beckley Blast Furnace on your left, just before crossing over the Blackberry River.

The dam and falls are directly upstream, visible from the parking area, only 100 feet away. There is much to observe and learn at this rare outdoor museum.

4

FALLS AT SAGES RAVINE

Location: Joyceville (Litchfield County), Sages Ravine
Delorme Connecticut/Rhode Island Atlas and Gazetteer: p. 49, A19; **Estimated GPS:** 42°03.00'N; 73°25.57'W
Views: Head-on, lateral
Aesthetics: Excellent
Characteristics: Scenic, wild, multiple cascades

Accessibility: First fall—0.3-mile hike; second fall—0.35-mile hike/scramble from start; third fall—0.4-mile hike/scramble from start
Degree of Difficulty: To first fall, moderately difficult; to second fall, difficult; to third fall, very difficult

DESCRIPTION: Multiple waterfalls have formed in a spectacular gorge called Sages Ravine. Covering a distance of over 1.0 mile, Sages Ravine Brook drops nearly 700 feet through a tortuous, chiseled defile, plunging over a series of large waterfalls and hidden pools, all encased in a forest of hemlocks. It is a very primordial area.

The first waterfall, near the bottom of the ravine, is 10 feet high and part of a grouping of several cascades. The second fall is an 8-foot-high, multistep fall that drops into a shallow pool. The third waterfall, called Twin Falls, consists of a 35-foot-high cascade which drops into a pothole-formed pool, immediately followed by a 25-foot-high, diagonally inclined cascade. A number of smaller waterfalls are interspersed between the main ones as well as further upstream.

There are also cascades on Sages Ravine Brook downstream from the ravine. Directly below the CT 41 bridge spanning Sages Ravine Brook is a 15-foot-high cascade where the ruins of an old mill or bridge abutment wall are evident along its north bank.

HISTORY: Sages Ravine is named after the Sage family who were heavily involved in the area during the nineteenth century. Simeon Sage founded

First waterfall encountered in Sages Ravine

the Sage Iron Company, and the area quickly became known as Sage's Forge, only to change to Joyce's Forge when purchased later by John D. Joyce.

The most prominent member of the Sage family was Zachias (also spelled Zaccheus) Sage, a Revolutionary War solider who is interred in the nearby Candee-Sage's Cemetery.

Henry Ward Beecher was so impressed by the ravine, particularly Twin Falls, that he publicized the natural wonder in his "State Papers" during the 1850s.

Today the Salisbury Land Trust and the Nature Conservancy safeguard Sages Ravine.

DIRECTIONS: From Salisbury (junction of CT 41 and US 44), drive north on CT 41 for 4.8 miles. Turn left into a small pullout for three or four cars just before crossing over the bridge spanning Sages Ravine Brook and reaching the Massachusetts/Connecticut border.

From South Egremont in Massachusetts (junction of MA 23 and MA 41), drive south on MA 41 for 8.0 miles and turn right into a small pull-out after crossing over Sages Ravine Brook.

Sages Ravine: From the parking area follow a path (initially an old road) west that parallels the south bank of Sages Ravine Brook. After nearly 0.3 mile of fairly level terrain you will come to the beginning of Sages Ravine. The first cascade is slightly upstream from this point and will require some scrambling to get to. You may notice one or two old blue-blaze markers— a carry-over from earlier days when a spur trail led from CT 41 up to the Appalachian National Scenic Trail before landslides and blowdown obliterated it.

In order to reach the second and third falls, you must be prepared for considerable scrambling, moving up and down along the side of the ravine over blowdown, boulders, and loose rock. This part of the trek should not be attempted by anyone who is unsure of their agility and sure-footedness.

The roadside cascade: Walk to the east side of the CT 41 bridge and look straight down over the top of a 15-foot-high cascade directly below. You can also go to the northeast end of the bridge and walk into the woods for 30 feet to see a lateral view of the cascade. Obey a sign posted by the Nature Conservancy stating ACCESS TO THIS AREA RESTRICTED. ECOLOGICAL EVALUATION IN PROGRESS, and go no further.

Two small cascades, just upstream, can be seen from the west side of the bridge.

ADDITIONAL CASCADE: At one time waterfallers frequently visited 25-foot-high Mt. Riga Falls, west of Salisbury. Readers already familiar with the fall should be advised that the area is now heavily posted, and no longer accessible to the public.

INTRODUCTION TO THE HOUSATONIC RIVER

The Housatonic River rises from four principal sources in western Massachusetts, draining a basin of 1,950 square miles, and flows a distance of 139 miles before emptying into Long Island Sound at Milford Point. Connecticut contains 83 of those miles, during which the river drops 645 feet. From Shelton to Long Island Sound the Housatonic becomes tidal, literally turning into a long arm of the Atlantic Ocean. Interestingly, because

Twin falls in Sages Ravine

the Housatonic spans a wider portion of the state, its Connecticut section is actually longer than that of the corresponding section of the Connecticut River.

Native Americans were the first to explore the Housatonic River. Seeing the mighty waterfall near Canaan, they called the river *pootatuck,* meaning "falls river." The first white man to sail up the Housatonic was the Dutch explorer Captain Adriaen Block, who accomplished the feat in 1614. Block called the Housatonic *rodenberg,* Dutch for "river of the red hills"—a reference to the color of the valley bedrock, a reddish hue produced by the underlying sandstone. Dutch seamen, who followed Block's route, called the river Westenhook. Later, boatmen who were obviously impressed by the river's immensity and power suggested the name "The Great River." None of these names stuck, however. Today we know the river as the Housatonic, derived from the Mohegan word *usi-a-di-en-uk* for "place beyond the mountains."

Despite the Dutch being the first Europeans to explore and settle the area, they were unable to establish a lasting foothold in the New World. Just as was true in New York State, they were ultimately squeezed out of power by the English who, by 1639, had established two plantations at the mouth of the Housatonic River.

Since these early days, the brute power of the Housatonic River has been repeatedly harnessed to power a variety of industries. The earliest of these were sawmills and gristmills.

Today a series of five dams and hydroelectric plants intercept the river, with locations at Falls Village, Bulls Bridge, Shepaug (which forms Lake Lillinonah), Stevenson (which forms Lake Zoar), and Derby (which forms Lake Housatonic).

South of Bulls Bridge, the first pump storage reservoir to be built in the United States—5,420-acre Lake Candlewood—diverts a portion of water from the Housatonic, pumping it uphill through a penstock. At nights, when energy demands are low, water is cheaply pumped uphill into the lake. At times when the Housatonic River runs at low volume and becomes anemic, the reservoir releases water to power the generators at the Rocky River Power Station just north of New Milford along US 7. You can see the huge pipes on the west side of the road opposite from the utility company.

Oliver Wendell Holmes, Sr., a physician, poet, writer, and the father of the famous U.S. Supreme Court justice, coined the phrase "There is no tonic like the Housatonic"—a slogan which still resonates today with hikers, fishing enthusiasts, and paddlers.

The Upper Housatonic Valley National Heritage Area (www.upper-housatonicheritage.org) watches over the region, working to "illuminate the diverse, rich identity of the Upper Housatonic River Valley region and to preserve and promote its historical, cultural and natural resources."

5

GREAT FALLS OF THE HOUSATONIC

Location: Northwest of Falls Village (Litchfield County)
Delorme Connecticut/Rhode Island Atlas and Gazetteer: p. 49, F23; **Estimated GPS:** Lower Parking Area—41°57.66'N; 73°22.44'W; Upper Parking Area—41°57.79'N; 73°22.41'W
Views: Lateral, close-up; head-on, distant
Aesthetics: Excellent
Characteristics: Urban, historic, broad, large, robust (at times)

Accessibility: Lateral view—100-foot walk; head-on view—0.2-mile hike along path paralleling the Housatonic River which provides fairly consistent upriver views; at one point a side trail descends to the streambed downriver from the fall, but involves a fairly demanding scramble
Degree of Difficulty: Easy to moderately easy

DESCRIPTION: The Great Falls of the Housatonic, aka Canaan Falls and Housatonic Falls, is on the Housatonic River. The waterfall is a massive, inclined block of Stockbridge marble, roughly 40–50 feet in height, and capped by a large dam. Viewed laterally, the waterfall seems considerably more inclined than when seen from afar. On the opposite side of the river you can see a gatehouse at the top of the falls. From here the Firstlight Power Resources' Falls Village Hydro Station (which you passed on the way up Water Street) diverts a significant portion of the river for its use 0.5 mile downstream.

Under conditions of normal flow, a 3-foot-high undercut in the bedrock is visible further downstream, about 0.1 mile from the falls, where the river has formed a cavity that goes back some 6 feet.

With the arrival of spring and snowmelt, the Great Falls becomes powerful and absolutely mesmerizing. Richard H. Beisel, Jr., creator of the

The Great Falls of the Housatonic River

International Waterfall Classification System, gives the Great Falls of the Housatonic a Class 5 rating—an impressive number for a Connecticut waterfall, although, to be sure, a rating that falls far short of a class 10 waterfall like Niagara Falls. Regrettably, the waterfall loses most of its luster after early spring as precious waters are bled off in great quantities for hydropower generation.

At one time a smaller, ledge-shaped waterfall, called Little Falls, could be seen upstream from the Great Falls, but it disappeared from sight when the dam was erected, impounding the river above the falls.

HISTORY: The Great Falls of the Housatonic was industrialized by the mid-1700s when harnessed to power a gristmill, bolting mill, fulling mill, paper mill, iron work, and blacksmith shop. In 1744 Burral's Bridge was erected over the Housatonic River a short distance downriver from the waterfall—the first to cross the upper section of the river.

In 1833 the Ames Iron Works was erected, which manufactured wheels and axles for locomotives, cannon and balls for the Civil War, and steamboat shafts. The nearby present-day community of Ames is named after this iron works.

Originally the village below the falls was called Canaan Falls. In 1841 a railroad line was established on the east side of the river. The train station was called "Falls Village," and soon after the town became known by that name.

In 1845 the Water Power Company was created to turn Falls Village into a manufacturing empire. A 3-mile power canal was completed in 1851, with the expectation being that numerous mills and factories would come to make use of the available hydropower. The blocks in the canal, however, had been set into place without cement mortar, causing the entire canal to leak like a sieve when the channel opened. The project ultimately ended up being a failure. Part of the canal's stone wall survives, however, and can be seen along Water Street, across the road from the Firstlight Power Resources' Falls Village Hydro Station.

In 1912 The Connecticut Lights and Power Company was formed by J. Henry Roraback of Canaan after obtaining rights to the falls from the Water Power Company and the New Haven Railroad Company. The hydroelectric plant became operational in 1914, producing 12,000 horsepower. The power company, today known as Firstlight Power Resources' Falls Village Hydro Station, is downriver from the Great Falls, just south of the one-lane bridge spanning the Housatonic River along the east bank of the river.

The upper Little Falls, now underwater, was once the site of Captain John Beebe's gristmill, circa 1742.

DIRECTIONS: From Canaan (junction of US 44 and US 7) proceed south, then southwest, on US 7 (South Canaan Road) for 5.9 miles. Along

HOUSATONIC FALLS, FALLS VILLAGE, CANAAN, CONN.

The Great Falls of the Housatonic River as it looked one hundred years ago (postcard)

the way you will pass by a roadside waterfall at 2.1 miles on your left behind a private residence (41°59.89'N; 73°19.72'W). The 30-foot-high cascade is on a tiny creek flowing out of the Housatonic State Forest into Robbins Swamp.

When you come to a flashing traffic light at 5.9 miles, turn right onto CT 126 (Main Street) and head west toward Falls Village. At 0.3 mile, bear left at a fork in the road, continuing west on Main Street. In another 0.2 mile, you will reach the end of Main Street. Turn right onto Railroad Street and then make a quick left (north) onto Water Street, going under a train overpass and then paralleling the Housatonic River. In 0.4 mile turn left onto a one-lane metal bridge and cross over the Housatonic River.

At the west end of the bridge, turn right onto Housatonic River Road (which parallels the river).

Downstream view and walk along river to waterfall: Drive 0.2 mile north on Housatonic River Road and pull into a small parking area on your right which is 0.2 mile downriver from the waterfall. Look directly across the road to view a cascading stream formed on a tiny tributary to the Housatonic River called Wetauwanchu Brook (41°57.66'N; 73°22.44'W).

Follow the white-blazed trail north along the west bank of the Housatonic River for 0.2 mile. In less than 0.1 mile, a steep side trail (involving a difficult scramble) leads down to the edge of the river, where excellent unobstructed views of the waterfall can be obtained.

Continue north on the main path for another 0.1 mile. The trail leads to the top of the waterfall, where several overlooks, including a main one with guardrails, give you clear views of the Great Falls from a variety of perspectives.

Main, lateral view of fall: Continue driving north on Housatonic River Road for a total of 0.4 mile from the bridge to a pullout on your right next to large boulders. From here follow a trail, which leads immediately to the top of the waterfall, where there are excellent lateral views. Most people stop to look at the Great Falls of the Housatonic here.

The white-blazed trail leads along the top of the gorge for several hundred feet north, as well as 0.2 mile south following along the rim of the gorge to the lower parking area.

About 50 feet beyond this pullout and upstream from the dam is a larger parking area to your right typically used by anglers and paddlers.

ADDITIONAL CASCADE #1: A narrow cascade on Wetauwanchu Brook, a small tributary to the Housatonic, can be seen opposite the lower parking area. Here a stream emanating from the southeast shoulder of Raccoon Hill races down the hillside on the west side of Housatonic River

Road, producing a number of small cascades before flowing into the Housatonic River. The main cascade is 15 feet high and roughly 200 feet into the woods from the road.

A number of tiny drops are visible directly where the creek flows under Housatonic River Road.

This cascade is best viewed in the early spring before the woods fill out with leaves and obscure the view.

ADDITIONAL CASCADE #2: A pretty 6-foot-high cascade can be seen on the Housatonic River 0.4 mile downstream from the Great Falls. From a pullout at the northwest end of the one-lane metal bridge spanning the Housatonic River (41°57.49'N; 73°22.26'W) follow a white-blazed trail north for over 0.05 mile, veering right at a fork. This side path takes you immediately down to the river to the base of the cascade. Look closely and you will see pieces of smelted iron, called "salamander rock," scattered about the trail near the river.

6

DEAN'S RAVINE FALLS

Location: North of West Cornwall (Litchfield County), Deans Ravine; Mohawk Trail

Delorme Connecticut/Rhode Island Atlas and Gazetteer: p. 50, H1; **Estimated GPS:** 41°55.10'N; 73°20.56'W

Views: Head-on, lateral

Aesthetics: Excellent

Characteristics: Remote, scenic, large

Accessibility: 0.3-mile hike

Degree of Difficulty: Moderate

Information: Trail map available in Ann T. Colson (ed.), *Connecticut Walk Book: The Guide to the Blue-Blazed Hiking Trails of Western Connecticut* (19th ed.), (Connecticut Forest & Park Association, 2006), page 211.

DESCRIPTION: Dean's Ravine Falls, aka Reed Brook Falls, is a 50-foot-high cascade in Dean's Ravine and on Reed Brook—a small stream that rises south of Yelping Hill in Cream Hollow, and flows into the Housatonic River west of Hough Mountain. Several smaller cascades can be seen before the main waterfall is encountered.

HISTORY: Dean's Ravine is a deep trench on the west shoulder of Music Mountain. The ravine has also been spelled Dean Ravine and Deane's Ravine, a name possibly attributable to John Dean, an early settler, or one of his six children.

At one time seven dams impounded Reed Brook. The stream is named after Hawley and Harry Reed, two brothers who bought a farm in the hollow at the foot of Bunker Hill.

DIRECTIONS: From Falls Village (junction of US 7 and CT 126), drive south on US 7 for 1.5 miles and turn left onto Lime Rock Station Road.

From West Cornwall (junction of US 7 and CT 128), go north on US 7 for 6.4 miles (or 0.3 mile past the junction of CT 112 and US 7), and turn right onto Lime Rock Station Road.

Coming from either direction follow Lime Rock Road south, taking note that the road becomes River Road along the way. At 1.0 mile, turn left onto Music Mountain Road and drive uphill, heading southeast. When you come to the intersection of Music Mountain Road and Cream Hill Road at 0.8 mile, turn quickly left into a parking area.

Proceeding on foot, follow the blue-blazed Mohawk Trail from the parking area, immediately turning left when you come to the ravine. The path, now paralleling the ravine, will quickly take you down to the level of Reed

Dean's Ravine Falls coming down the wall of the Housatonic Valley

Brook where a small cascade is visible upstream. Continue your walk downstream.

At 0.1 mile the ravine narrows markedly, compressing the stream. Several small cascades can be seen here. Looking downstream you will observe the brink of the main waterfall where Dean's Ravine opens up and drops dramatically 50 feet into a lower section of the gorge.

Continue following the blue-blazed trail as it passes by the top of the main waterfall to your right. Although the trail initially seems to lead away from the waterfall, it quickly switches back and descends to the bottom of the ravine where excellent views of the waterfall can be obtained.

If you follow the blue-blazed trail further downstream it will eventually intersect Music Mountain Road at a point downhill from where you parked.

To see additional falls on Reed Brook, return to the parking area and follow the blue-blazed trail upstream for 0.05 mile. The trail emerges onto Music Mountain Road. Walk over to the small bridge which spans Reed Brook. To your right is an 8-foot-high cascade; to your left, downstream, is a smaller cascade.

7

HATCH BROOK FALLS

Location: Northwest of Cornwall Bridge (Litchfield County), Housatonic Meadows State Park
Delorme Connecticut/Rhode Island Atlas and Gazetteer: p. 40, A10; **Estimated GPS:** 41°49.99'N; 73°23.00'W
Views: Lateral from top of bank, head-on from streambed
Aesthetics: Good

Characteristics: Remote, scenic, medium-sized
Accessibility: 0.2-mile hike
Degree of Difficulty: Moderate
Information: Housatonic Meadows State Park, 860-927-3238 or 1-866-287-2757; trail map available at http://www.ct.gov/dep/lib/dep/stateparks/maps/housatonic meadowstrailmap.pdf

DESCRIPTION: Hatch Brook Falls is a 30-foot-high cascade on Hatch Brook—a small stream which rises in the hills northwest of Cornwall Bridge and flows into the Housatonic River just east of US 7. The waterfall is in a small gorge whose north wall slopes enough to enable a hiker to scramble

Hatch Brook Falls, only a short distance upstream on Hatch Brook

down to the bottom of the ravine for a closer look. Due to its limited watershed, early spring or following heavy rainfall is the time to visit Hatch Brook Falls.

The brook and falls are likely named either for the abundance of mayflies and caddisflies that hatch here in the early spring—beneficiaries of the water's idyllic pH level that results from the streambed's underlying limestone deposits—or after Captain Ebenezer Hatch, who came to Sharon from Kent in 1768, and whose name has been given to a nearby pond where a puddling works once melted down pig iron to rid it of slag.

HISTORY: Cornwall Bridge was earlier known as Deantown after Reuben Dean who built the town's first mill, named Red Mill, around 1750. Like West Cornwall, Cornwall Bridge became heavily involved in smelting iron during the nineteenth century. The cumulative effect of this industry on the environment, however, was devastating. Forests were reduced to fields of rotting stumps as trees in increasing numbers were harvested to produce charcoal—a concentrated form of energy which generated the intense heat that the forges required. Once the forests were gone, the days of charcoal production were numbered.

DIRECTIONS: From Cornwall Bridge (junction of US 7 and CT 4), drive northwest on US 7 for over 1.0 mile. Pull into a parking area on your left just before crossing over Hatch Brook. You will see a sign next to the road that states BLUE PINE KNOB TRAIL LOOP.

Approaching from West Cornwall (junction of US 7 and CT 128) drive south on US 7 for 3.1 miles and turn right into a parking area.

The short hike follows a trail frequently used by hikers who set out on the 2.5-mile-long Pine Knob Loop.

From the side of the parking area follow the blue-blazed trail north for several hundred feet. Rock hop over Hatch Brook via several large stepping-stones, and turn left at the top of the ravine. Follow the trail uphill for 0.2 mile, paralleling Hatch Brook, which stays to your left. When you come to several mammoth boulders deeply embedded in the earth, turn left and make your way down the side of the ravine and over to the base of the falls. Since there is no formal path, a short 50- to 75-foot scramble will be necessary.

If you wish, lateral views of the cascade can be obtained from the top of the ravine, roughly a hundred feet further uphill past the boulders.

In another 0.1 mile the blue-blazed trail descends to nearly the same level as the streambed, where a 20-foot-long waterslide can be seen. It is not tilted vertically enough, however, to qualify as a cascade.

Pine Swamp Brook Falls—a roadside wonder that is passed in the blink of an eye

ADDITIONAL CASCADE: Pine Swamp Brook Falls (41°51.98'N; 73°22.18'W) is a 25-foot-high, two-tier waterfall on Pine Swamp Brook— a small stream which rises from east of Mine Mountain and flows into the Housatonic River southwest of West Cornwall.

From West Cornwall (junction of US 7 and CT 128) go south on US 7 for 0.5 mile. From west of Cornwall Bridge (junction of US 7 and CT 4), drive north on US 7 for 3.6 miles.

Approaching from either direction, look for the waterfall tucked away in a narrow slot in the rock wall along the west side of the road. The waterfall can only be glimpsed fleetingly from the roadside, however, unless you park in a pullout 100 feet from the falls and walk back carefully, hugging the guardrail and watching out for cars.

8

KENT FALLS

Location: Northeast of North
Kent (Litchfield County), Kent Falls
State Park
**Delorme Connecticut/Rhode
Island Atlas and Gazetteer:**
p. 40, E9; **Estimated GPS:**
41°46.57'N; 73°25.16'W
Views: Head-on, lateral
Aesthetics: Excellent
Characteristics: Historic, scenic,
large
Accessibility: 0.2-mile walk up
trail to uppermost falls

Degree of Difficulty: Moderately
easy to moderate depending upon
the height of your ascent
Information: Kent Falls State
Park, 860-927-3238; trail map
available at www.ct.gov/dep/cwp
/view.asp?a=2716&q=325228
Fee: Modest charge on weekends
and holidays from May through
October; out-of-state residents are
charged a slightly larger fee

DESCRIPTION: Kent Falls consist of a series of impressive cascades and drops formed on Kent Falls Brook, aka Falls Brook—a medium-sized stream which rises in the hills east of Wyantenock State Forest and flows into the Housatonic River a short distance downstream from the falls. Numerous pools and potholes can be seen in addition to the falls. The stream, which drains an area of 6–7 square miles, descends over 250 feet in less than 0.2 mile.

Approaching the base of Kent Falls, visitors can see four separate cascades, the first two being formed in Stockbridge marble. At the base of the lowest falls is a shallow wading pool.

Additional cascades are encountered as you hike further upstream, culminating near the top with a 15-foot drop into a large pothole historically known as the Maidens Well. Just below it is a 20-foot-high cascade where the waters continue their downward course. The two together are frequently photographed by tourists. Look closely and you will notice the image of a dog's head profiled in the rocks.

A number of potholes are prominently displayed in the bedrock near the waterfalls.

Several smaller waterfalls are further upstream near the confluence of Kent Falls Brook and a tributary of nearly equal size, but these are outside the park and on private land.

The image of a dog's head manifests itself at upper Kent Falls.

Lower Kent Falls

HISTORY: Many consider Kent Falls the "jewel of the inland parks." The waterfall is in the 295-acre Kent Falls State Park, created in 1919 through a gift of 200 acres of land from Alain White to the State of Connecticut. Since then additional parcels of land have been acquired.

Although little sign of past industrialization exists today, Kent Falls Brook was populated by a variety of mills during colonial times.

In the 1930s, the Civil Works Administration set about to develop the area, assigning the work to Camp Macedonia Company #1191. Although the work was completed according to plan, by the 1970s the park was already in need of a serious upgrade, and the Youth Conservation Corps of Connecticut took on the project of revitalizing the park.

Despite all of this, in 2006 still more renovations were needed, and an additional $1.1 million was approved. New viewing platforms were created, the trail was redesigned, and a terraced observation area was made out of native flagstone next to the wading pool at the bottom of the falls.

Kent Falls achieved minor celebrity status when it served as background for a show on TV's long-running soap opera the *Guiding Light*.

In 1974 Edmund Palmer, a park employee, built the 37-foot-long Town Lattice Truss covered bridge that crosses Kent Falls Brook at the beginning of the trail.

A reproduction of a painting of Kent Falls by Willard Metcalf, a well-known nineteenth century American Impressionist, decorates an on-site historic plaque.

DIRECTIONS: From Cornwall Bridge (junction of US 7 and CT 4) drive southwest on US 7 for 3.9 miles. Turn left into Kent Falls State Park.

From Kent (junction of US 7 and CT 341), drive northeast on US 7 for 5.0 miles and turn right into the park.

From the north end of the parking area, follow the main trail over a covered footbridge and then across an open field to the base of the lowermost falls. From here, it is an ascent of over 250 feet following a well-constructed, inlaid stone trail, with periodic platform overlooks and a railing made of thin cable that is neither obtrusive nor unduly offensive.

9

MACEDONIA GORGE AND FALLS

Location: North of Macedonia (Litchfield County), Macedonia Brook State Park

Delorme Connecticut/Rhode Island Atlas and Gazetteer: p. 40, F4; **Estimated GPS:** 41°45.21'N; 73°29.58'W

Views: Head-on, lateral

Aesthetics: Fair

Characteristics: Remote, historic, small

Accessibility: Visible from top of ravine, or by following a short trail that leads down to old mill ruins in several hundred feet

Degree of Difficulty: Moderately easy

Information: Macedonia Brook State Park, 860-927-3238; trail map available at www.ct.gov/dep/cwp /view.asp?a=2716&q=325234

Fee: None for visiting the waterfall; campsite fee only

Hours: Campsites are open from mid-April to September 30th; 51 sites available

DESCRIPTION: The falls in Macedonia Gorge are on Macedonia Brook, a comparatively small stream which rises in the West Wood area and flows into the Housatonic River by Kent.

The falls consist of a series of small cascades, none greater than 3–4 feet in height, which extend through a 100-foot-long ravine where the bedding is noticeably tilted. The stone ruins of an old forge can be seen by the base of the lowermost cascade where a small pool of water has formed. Flakes of iron ore are noticeable along the path that leads downhill to the ruins.

A small cascade 0.4 mile further upstream can also be seen. Like the ones in Macedonia Gorge, this falls is relatively unobtrusive. It is on the left side of the road in a fairly scenic area where picnic tables overlook the ravine.

HISTORY: The falls in Macedonia Gorge are in Macedonia Brook State Park, a 2,294-acre preserve containing 13 miles of trails. The park's main stream, Macedonia Brook, has also been known as Nodine Hollow Brook and Forge Brook in the past.

Macedonia Brook State Park's history dates back to 1918 when 1,552 acres of land were gifted to the State of Connecticut by the White Memorial Foundation of Litchfield. During the 1930s the Civilian Conservation Corps (CCC) became heavily involved in shaping the way the park looks today.

The name Macedonia comes from the biblical Book of Acts where the Lord is asked to "Come into Macedonia and help us."

The Schaghticoke originally occupied the area near Macedonia Gorge. The tribe's name refers to the confluence of the Housatonic River and nearby Tenmile River.

The nearby village of Kent was settled in 1738. Macedonia quickly followed and soon was bustling with shops that included a cider mill, sawmill, and gristmill. But it was for its foundries that Macedonia was best known, starting between 1770 and 1773, when an iron works was erected on Macedonia Brook.

In 1826 the blast furnaces at Macedonia began smelting iron ore to convert cast iron into malleable iron, producing crowbars, agricultural implements, wagon wheel rims, and other metal-based items.

By 1848 all the timber in the immediate area had been harvested, forcing the iron companies to import timber from ever-expanding distances. It was undoubtedly the loss of easily obtained local timber and the resulting need to harvest large quantities from widening distances which led to the furnaces closing in 1865, along with the stiff business competition from the larger Pennsylvania mines. Today you can still see the remains of the forge and stamping works at the south end of the park.

DIRECTIONS: From Kent (junction of US 7 and CT 341), head northwest on CT 341 (which starts off as Bridge Street) for 1.8 miles until you come to a sign for Macedonia Brook State Park. Turn right onto Macedonia Brook Road and drive north for 1.0 mile. You will see, to your left, a kiosk where the park's rules and regulations are posted. Park at a sizable pullout to your right. From here a series of small cascades can be seen from the top of the ravine. For a better look, follow a short trail down into the gorge for upstream views of the cascades.

A second, solitary cascade is at 1.4 miles. You will see it down in the ravine on the left side of the road.

Although Macedonia Brook Road and, further uphill, Keeler Road can be followed north for roughly 4 miles, there are no further cascades. Still, this is a wonderful camping area, particularly if you are interested in doing a variety of hikes or summiting 1,380-foot-high Cobble Mountain.

The ranger's cabin/park office is at 1.9 miles as you proceed into Macedonia Brook State Park.

10

THAYER BROOK CASCADES

Location: Southwest of Kent (Litchfield County), Appalachian National Scenic Trail **Delorme Connecticut/Rhode Island Atlas and Gazetteer:** p. 40, H4; **Estimated GPS:** 41°43.83'N; 73°29.39'W **Views:** Head-on, lateral **Aesthetics:** Fair **Characteristics:** Remote, seasonal, small

Accessibility: 1.3-mile hike **Degree of Difficulty:** Difficult **Information:** Trail map available in Ann T. Colson (ed.), *Connecticut Walk Book: The Guide to the Blue-Blazed Hiking Trails of Western Connecticut* (19th ed.), (Connecticut Forest & Park Association, 2006), page 34.

DESCRIPTION: A pretty 6-foot-high cascade has formed roughly 0.1 mile downstream from where the Appalachian National Scenic Trail crosses over Thayer Brook—a small stream which rises from a marshy area in the mountains west of Kent and flows into the Housatonic River south of Kent.

HISTORY: Thayer Brook is named after the Thayer family who were long-term area residents.

The Appalachian National Scenic Trail, which passes near the cascade, extends from Springer Mountain in Georgia to Mt. Katahdin in Maine, a distance of 2,175 miles. From 1929 to 1932, Ned K. Anderson, Connecticut Forest and Park Association chair of the Housatonic Valley section, laid out the portion of the trail in Connecticut that covers 52 miles of mountainous terrain.

DIRECTIONS: From Kent (junction of US 7 and CT 341), drive northwest on CT 341 for 0.8 mile. Look for a pullout on your left where the Appalachian National Scenic Trail crosses CT 341.

Follow the white-blazed Appalachian National Scenic Trail south for 1.3 miles until you come to Thayer Brook. The first part of the hike is a continuous ascent up the "Grand Staircase" to the top of Mt. Algo, and then down into a notch formed between Mt. Algo (1,175 feet) and an adjacent mountain (1,403 feet).

Where the Appalachian National Scenic Trail crosses Thayer Brook is a tiny 2- to 3-foot-high cascade. Follow the north bank of the brook downstream for 0.1 mile until you come to a pretty, 6-foot-high cascade. Although technically a bushwhack, hikers need merely retrace their steps, following the brook back upstream, to reach the trail again.

It makes sense to visit this small cascade only if you are already hiking on the Appalachian National Scenic Trail.

11

CASCADES ALONG SCHAGHTICOKE ROAD

Location: Between Kent and Bulls Bridge (Litchfield County), Schaghticoke Indian Reservation
Delorme Connecticut/Rhode Island Atlas and Gazetteer: p. 40, J3–14; **Estimated GPS:** South-most cascade—41°41.43'N; 73°30.33'W; North-most cascade—41°41.85'N; 73°29.98'W
Views: Head-on
Aesthetics: Fair
Characteristics: Remote, medium-sized
Accessibility: Roadside

DESCRIPTION: Two seasonal cascades can be found along Schaghticoke Road which are pretty to view in the early spring, but which quickly diminish in size and luster with the arrival of summer. Both are by the Schaghticoke Indian Reservation, and both are near terminuses of streams that quickly end up flowing into the Housatonic River.

The southmost cascade is 30 feet high, and races down a near-vertical slope of bedrock by the road. The stream breaks up at the top of the cliff into several rivulets which cascade separately down the rock face. At the base of the cliff the rivulets are reunited, the reformed stream channels under the road, and immediately flows into the Housatonic River.

The northmost cascade is further into the woods, making it harder to see from the roadside—particularly if you are visiting when the trees are leaf-bearing. The cascade is 35 feet high and on a stream which carries slightly more water than the southmost cascade.

Less than 0.1 mile further north is a small cascade behind a private home which is also visible from the roadside.

HISTORY: The Schaghticokes, a Native American tribe whose name refers to the confluence of the Housatonic River and nearby Tenmile River, occupy the Schaghticoke Indian Reservation. The reservation, granted to the tribe in 1736, encompasses 400 acres of land (but at one time covered 2,500 acres). It is reputed to be one of the oldest reservations in North America.

During the Revolutionary War, one hundred members of the tribe contributed to the war effort by scouting and serving in the signal corps where drums and smoke fires could be used to relay messages faster than the fleetest rider on horseback. The smoke signals proved particularly successful, using a code that the British were never able to crack.

DIRECTIONS: Schaghticoke Road parallels the west bank of the Housatonic River between Kent and Bulls Bridge, providing a scenic ride as it follows along the base of high cliffs near the road's south end.

From Kent (junction of US 7 and CT 341) drive northwest on CT 341 (Bridge Street) for 0.7 mile, and turn left onto Schaghticoke Road, heading south. In 2.4 miles you will pass by the first cascade in the woods off to your right. It can be difficult to see. At 3.1 miles, the second cascade will be visible from the roadside and also on your right. At 4.2 miles you will reach Bulls Bridge Road.

Approaching from Gaylordsville (junction of CT 55 and US 7), drive northwest on US 7 for 2.6 miles. Turn left onto Bulls Bridge Road and drive west for 0.3 mile, crossing over the east and west channels of the Housatonic River. When you come to Schaghticoke Road, turn right and head north. In 1.1 miles you will reach a small cascade visible from the roadside on your left. At 1.8 mile, you will pass by a less obtrusive cascade, set some 70 feet into the woods, also on your left. At over 4.2 miles you will come to CT 341.

This is a road well worth driving on, not only because of its waterfalls, but because of its views of the Housatonic River and the Schaghticoke Indian Reservation with its historic cemetery and houses with unique architecture.

12

BULLS BRIDGE CASCADES

Location: Bulls Bridge (Litchfield County), Bulls Bridge Scenic Area
Delorme Connecticut/Rhode Island Atlas and Gazetteer: p. 40, K3; **Estimated GPS:** 41°40.54'N; 73°30.61'W
Views: Head-on, lateral
Aesthetics: Fair

Characteristics: Historic, scenic, small
Accessibility: Less than 0.05-mile walk to cascades, 0.1- to 0.3-mile walk to artificial waterfalls created by dams
Degree of Difficulty: Easy

DESCRIPTION: The cascades at Bulls Bridge are formed on the Housatonic River in an area familiar to white-water paddlers. Particularly troublesome spots have yielded such colorful appellations as Stairway to Hell (which is 20 feet long and choked with boulders), Threshold (30+ feet long), The Flume (7 feet long), S-Turn, and The Pencil Sharpener. This stretch of the Housatonic can be very dangerous due to fast-moving waters over rocks and boulders. Stay a safe distance back from the water's edge.

Although much white water and several cascades are evident at Bulls Bridge, none are of major size, nor are any vigorously animated during most of the year. The reason for this is that a sluiceway running along the east bank (which you drove over just before crossing the covered bridge) diverts a significant portion of the Housatonic River south, initially by the sluiceway and later by penstock, to a hydroelectric plant some 2 miles downriver.

The first waterfall encountered is a small cascade below a dam on the right just upstream from Bulls Bridge. A fairly robust, constant flow of water is maintained here compared to the residue that generally remains to nourish the river's east and west channels.

Look upriver to the left of the dam and cascade and you will see the riverbed choked with boulders and sculptured rocks, all in a comparative state of dryness. Generally little water flows down this way except during times of high water.

Your attention will also be drawn to the weirdly shaped bedrock just upstream from the bridge. The streambed is literally filled with potholes and sculpted rocks of all sizes and shapes—a veritable moonscape. One large pothole near the bridge is shaped like a carnival saucer ride, 6 feet deep and 8 feet in diameter.

The cascades and rapids downstream from Bulls Bridge are easily observed from a wooden platform at the south end of the island. A 3-foot-high cascade visible just downriver is particularly noteworthy. To the right of the viewing platform is the west channel of the Housatonic, containing a 40-foot-long, narrow, flumelike channel. Here the stream is momentarily compressed. Although the cascade—called The Flume—is probably no more than 4 feet high, the streambed is notably tilted, giving the racing waters a dramatic look. Steps next to the wooden platform lead down to The Flume for those who wish to see the cascade close-up. Be careful here, for the waters are fast-moving. About 30 feet from the platform overlook, a 20-foot-long path leads east to an overlook of a 3- to 4-foot-high cascade on the river's east section.

As you can see by looking at a *Delorme Connecticut/Rhode Island Atlas and Gazetteer,* Bulls Bridge is near the Connecticut and New York border. A section of the Appalachian National Scenic Trail, which crosses over into New York State temporarily to negotiate 1,331-foot-high Schaghticoke Mountain, is close at hand and provides superlative views of the Housatonic River Gorge (see next entry).

HISTORY: Bulls Bridge and the tiny community which once thrived here are named after Jacob Bull of Dover, New York, who, along with his brother, established a gristmill and ironworks around 1740. William Johnson and David Lewis built the first Bulls Bridge in 1777.

BULL'S BRIDGE, KENT, CONN. ONE OF THE FEW
OLD COVERED BRIDGES LEFT IN CONNECTICUT.

This covered bridge lends Bulls Bridge its name (ca. 1940 postcard).

Flume Cascade at Bulls Bridge

During the Revolutionary War, General George Washington is said to have led his troops over the bridge on at least four different occasions. A widely recounted story has it that he inadvertently fell into the stream on one of the crossings. Exactly how this happened has been a subject of much debate.

In 1826 a furnace was erected at Bulls Bridge.

The present 109-foot-long, one-span town lattice and queen post trust covered bridge was built in 1842. Plate girders were installed beneath the deck in 1969 to provide reinforcement. Only three traditional covered bridges remain in Connecticut today, and two of them are on the Housatonic River, one at Bulls Bridge and the other at West Cornwall. The third, known as the Comstock Covered Bridge, is east of the Connecticut River in East Hampton. Today, Bulls Bridge is listed on the National Register of Historic Places.

In 1917 the Connecticut Light and Power Company established the Rocky River Power Station at Bulls Bridge. The Bulls Bridge Scenic Area is open to the public thanks to the civic-mindedness of Firstlight Power Resources.

DIRECTIONS: From Kent (junction of US 7 and CT 341) drive southwest on US 7 for 3.9 miles and turn right onto Bulls Bridge Road.

From Gaylordsville (junction of CT 55 and US 7) head northwest on US 7 for 2.6 miles. Then turn left onto Bulls Bridge Road.

From either direction, proceed west on Bulls Bridge Road for 0.1 mile, crossing over the single-lane covered bridge which spans the Housatonic River, and then turn immediately right into a parking area designated BULLS BRIDGE SCENIC AREA.

Although it may not be apparent at first, you have just set foot onto a 0.3-mile-long island, formed where the river has been split into two channels. Both are dammed, causing water levels to vary considerably.

To visit the upper cascade, walk over to the kiosk from the parking area and then follow a path leading down to the riverbed next to Bulls Bridge. From here you can work your way upstream along the bedding and boulders for 50–70 feet for close-up views of the potholes, cascade, and the dam; or you can follow a path upstream along the top of the ravine for 100 feet to obtain views of the ravine, cascade, and dam.

To visit the lower cascade, walk south from the parking lot across the road and follow a path for less than 200 feet to the south end of the island. Here a wooden platform overlooks the river, and a short path to your right leads down to the streambed.

About 30 feet before the platform overlook, a short path to your left leads to views of a small cascade spanning the Housatonic River's east channel.

If you walk northwest for 100 feet from the platform overlook, you will come to a bridge spanning the river's west channel. Looking upstream from the north side of the bridge, you will see a series of small cascades culminating in a medium-sized dam. Watch out for cars while on the bridge.

If you wish to visit several artificial waterfalls (dams erected on the Housatonic River at Bulls Bridge), follow the canoe portage trail, a dirt road, north from the kiosk. In less than 0.05 mile you will come to a side path leading off to your left. It quickly leads you to a 10-foot-high dam and views of the west channel of the Housatonic. Below the dam are rapids—at best, quasi cascades.

Return to the canoe portage trail and continue north. In 0.2 mile you will reach the north end of the island where the trail divides: going left will take you to a canoe access point upstream from the west channel dam; going right will lead you in less than 0.05 mile to the east channel dam.

13

HOUSATONIC RIVER GORGE AND CASCADES

Location: South of Bulls Bridge (Litchfield County), Appalachian National Scenic Trail

Delorme Connecticut/Rhode Island Atlas and Gazetteer: p. 40, K3; **Estimated GPS:** 41°40.51'N; 73°30.66'W

Views: Lateral, looking down and across from rim of gorge

Aesthetics: Good

Characteristics: Remote, scenic, small

Accessibility: 0.8-mile hike with continuous views

Degree of Difficulty: Moderate

Information: Trail map available in Ann T. Colson (ed.), *Connecticut Walk Book: The Guide to the Blue-Blazed Hiking Trails of Western Connecticut* (19th ed.), (Connecticut Forest & Park Association, 2006), pages 32–33.

DESCRIPTION: A number of cascades and rapids have formed on the Housatonic River along an 0.8-mile-long section called the Housatonic

Small cascades on this section of the Housatonic River—a white-water paddler's paradise

River Gorge. This should not be confused with a similarly named area of the Housatonic River south of New Milford.

Be prepared for thrilling views looking down into the interior of the gorge from heights of over 100 feet. At one point a cascading stream next to a private home is visible on the opposite side of the gorge.

The 120-foot-long Anderson Memorial Bridge spanning the Tenmile River is the turnaround point (for this hike at least) after a one-way trek of 0.8 mile.

HISTORY: The Anderson Memorial Bridge was built in 1983 in honor of Ned K. Anderson, a Sherman farmer who laid out the Connecticut portion of the Appalachian National Scenic Trail and then maintained it for twenty years.

DIRECTIONS: From Kent (junction of US 7 and CT 341) drive southwest on US 7 for 3.9 miles and turn right onto Bulls Bridge Road.

From Gaylordsville (junction of CT 55 and US 7) head northwest on US 7 for 2.6 miles. Then turn left onto Bulls Bridge Road.

From either approach, drive west on Bulls Bridge Road for over 0.1 mile and park to your left as soon as you cross over the second channel of the Housatonic River. Follow the spur path southeast, paralleling the river, for less than 0.2 mile to reach the white-blazed Appalachian National Scenic Trail. The Appalachian National Scenic Trail follows high along the west bank of the Housatonic Gorge, providing spectacular views of the gorge, rapids, cascades, and potholes rounded out in the bedrock.

Before reaching the Appalachian National Scenic Trail, however, you can obtain excellent views, looking back upriver, of a 3- to 4-foot-high, flumelike cascade formed on the west channel of the Housatonic, a small cascade on the east channel of the Housatonic, and a broad 3- to 4-foot-high cascade that spans the entire river 100 feet downriver from Bulls Bridge island. Side paths lead down to close-up views of the flume cascade and downstream cascade.

At 0.5 mile into the hike you will see a 2-foot-high cascade in the riverbed. Just downstream, a cascading stream near a private residence falls steeply down the east bank into the river. The tiny cascades and rapids are nearly continuous until you reach Tenmile River. Turn around at the Anderson footbridge.

14

ASPETUCK FALLS

Location: New Preston (Litchfield County)
Delorme Connecticut/Rhode Island Atlas and Gazetteer: p. 40, K12; **Estimated GPS:** 41°40.52'N; 73°21.30'W

Views: Head-on
Aesthetics: Good
Characteristics: Urban, historic, medium-sized
Accessibility: Roadside

DESCRIPTION: Aspetuck Falls, aka New Preston Falls, is a 20-foot-high waterfall on the East Aspetuck River—a medium-sized stream which rises from Lake Waramaug at an elevation of 694 feet and joins with the West Aspetuck River south of Wellsville before flowing into the Housatonic River at New Milford.

Old foundations are visible along the east bank at the base of the falls, possibly the ruins of a stone sawmill once used for cutting slabs of rock for monuments.

HISTORY: At one time New Preston was a viable industrial center, using the power of the East Aspetuck River to run a total of 21 mills, including a

Aspetuck Falls, the centerpiece of New Preston

tannery, forge, twine and cotton factory, cider/brandy distillery, and carpentry shop. Originally the village was known as New Purchase, but an early settler named Edward Cogswell changed the name to New Preston in honor of his hometown of Preston in east Connecticut.

Lake Waramaug, encompassing 680 acres, is directly north of New Preston, and is the state's second largest natural body of water. The East Aspetuck River, rising from this lake, passes through Tinker Hill Gorge, aka Marks Hollow, where multiple dams intercept the river before it reaches New Preston and Aspetuck Falls. Lake Waramaug's name comes from a Native American who was chief of the Wyantenock tribe.

Aspetuck is a Paugussett word for "height," "high places," or "fishnet place," the former two presumably referring to the surrounding hillsides.

DIRECTIONS: From New Milford (junction of US 202 and CT 67) drive northeast on US 202 for approximately 7.5 miles to New Preston. Turn left onto CT 45 (East Shore Road) and drive north for less than 0.1 mile to a small parking area on your left where excellent views of Aspetuck Falls, just a short distance upstream, can be obtained from a stone platform overlook.

15

SITE OF THE "GREAT FALLS OF NEW MILFORD"

Location: New Milford (Litchfield County), Lovers Leap State Park
Delorme Connecticut/Rhode Island Atlas and Gazetteer: p. 31, G21; **Estimated GPS:** 41°32.64'N; 73°24.47'W
Views: Lateral view of site of the Great Falls (now underwater); interior views of the Housatonic Gorge from the east rim trail
Aesthetics: Excellent (gorge)
Characteristics: Historic

Accessibility: 0.05-mile walk to site of the former Bridgeport Wood Furnishing Company overlooking the Great Falls (now underwater); 0.3-mile walk to Lovers Leap overlook
Degree of Difficulty: Great Falls—easy; Lovers Leap—moderately easy
Information: Lovers Leap State Park, 203-797-4165; trail map: http://www.ct.gov/dep/lib/dep/state parks/maps/loversleap.pdf

DESCRIPTION: The Great Falls of New Milford—aka New Milford's Great Falls, Eel Rocks, Fishing Falls, Bridgewater Falls, and Lovers Leap Falls—no longer exists as a surface feature. The waterfall, along with Goodyear Island further south, was put underwater when the Housatonic River was dammed up to form an elongated, riverlike reservoir.

Native Americans called the falls *metichawan,* meaning "obstruction" or point of "turning back." It was here that large fish were blocked from continuing upriver. The waterfall is described as having been 17 feet high. Geologists believe it may once have been as high as 100 feet before the weight of countless centuries eroded it down. Today these erosive processes have slowed down significantly, and will only speed up again if the river is undammed and the falls brought back to life.

HISTORY: The Great Falls of New Milford is roughly 40 miles upriver from the Housatonic River's outflow at Long Island Sound. According to archaeologists, Native Americans were active at the falls during a span of over eight thousand years. At one time the great chief Waramaug established his "palace," a place of special residence, near the waterfall. Waramaug's palace was constructed out of bark with the smooth side facing inward so that the interior walls could be painted with figures of fish and beasts.

Native Americans came each year to fish for lamprey eels and shad, sea creatures that were in great abundance then at the popular waterfall site.

Downstream from the site of the Great Falls the river flows through a narrow chasm whose walls are nearly vertical. Lovers Leap, a high cliff overlook, can be found at the chasm's southwest corner. The name came from a supposed incident involving Chief Waramaug's only daughter, Princess Lillinonah, who leaped off the precipice with her ostracized white-skin lover rather than face life apart. There are many variations of this story, to be sure. Another version has Princess Lillinonah leaping into the river to drown herself after presuming her lover dead after his failure to return home at the expected time. Naturally, her lover is quite alive and arrives just in time to see the princess leaping to her death. Without forethought he jumps off Lovers Leap to save her, and dies as well. Such stories are endless variations of Romeo and Juliet, and are commonly associated with large waterfalls.

The initial 52 acres of Lovers Leap State Park were bequeathed to the state of Connecticut in 1971 by Catherine Hurd. Since then the park has expanded to 160 acres.

The Berlin Iron Bridge Company of Berlin, Connecticut, built the lenticular truss Falls Bridge spanning the north end of the gorge in 1895. Downstream from the Housatonic Gorge the river opens up into a broad basin called the Cove. Goodyear Island, named after Stephen Goodyear, once served as a handy seventeenth century trading post where furs were liberally exchanged. With the creation of 1,900-acre Lake Lillinonah in 1955 by Connecticut Light and Power, the island disappeared beneath the lake waters.

DIRECTIONS: From New Milford (junction of US 7 and US 202), go south on US 7/202 (Danbury Road) for 0.7 mile. Turn left onto Pickett District Road and drive south for 1.9 miles. At the stoplight turn left onto Still River Road and head northeast. Still River Road quickly merges into Pumpkin Hill Road. In 0.2 mile you will cross over the Still River. In 0.4 mile, just before reaching the Housatonic Gorge, turn right into Lovers Leap State Park and park 0.05 mile up the road in the main parking area. Walk over to the kiosk, which contains a general map of the area.

To site of the Bridgeport Wood Furnishing Company next to the now-buried Great Falls: Follow the paved road east from the kiosk past a series of historic plaques which lead immediately to the historic 1895 Falls Bridge. Before crossing the bridge, bear left and follow a path which leads down and under the west end of the Charles H. Marsh Memorial traffic bridge. You will immediately come out to the site of the Bridgeport Wood

Furnishing Company, whose foundation ruins remain standing today. Extending from the west bank is part of a dam that presumably once spanned the top of the Great Falls. You will see a line of rapids crossing the river, suggestive of what may lie below.

To historic Falls Bridge: From the kiosk follow the paved road east for several hundred feet to the Falls Bridge, which has not been used by automobile traffic for many decades. The bridge spans the gorge, providing superlative views to the south of the chasm's interior and, to the north, of the site of the Great Falls.

To Housatonic Gorge: From the parking area, walk east toward the gorge for several hundred feet and follow the blue-blazed trail south as it parallels the west rim. The path provides ongoing views of the chasm. In 0.2 mile the trail leads past the Indian Spring House, an old stone structure now in a state of collapse, then up and over a nubble to Lovers Leap at 0.3 mile. Lovers Leap is a frighteningly high overlook at the south end of the chasm. Extreme caution should be exercised when approaching the edge for a view.

ADDITIONAL CASCADE #1: From Lovers Leap State Park, continue east across the Charles H. Marsh Memorial Bridge which spans the Housatonic Gorge. When you reach the east end of the bridge, turn left onto Grove Road and head north for 0.3 mile. Just before you reach Hine Hill Road on your right you will pass by a seasonal, 15-foot-high cascade adjacent to a private residence (41°32.99'N; 73°24.34'W). There is no way to stop for a close look, so just be content with a quick drive-by look.

ADDITIONAL CASCADE #2: It is also possible to stop at a series of small cascades and rapids on the Still River while driving to Lovers Leap State Park. When you come to the traffic light at the end of Pickett District Road, instead of turning left onto Still River Road continue straight ahead for 0.1 mile. You will see a gated entrance to 41-acre Harrybrooke Park on your left where limited parking space is available. Park next to the gate and walk less than 50 feet to the bridge spanning the Still River for upstream views of the cascades, where David Griswold established a gristmill in the 1710s.

16

CAROLINE GLEN CASCADE

Location: Roxbury (Litchfield County), Emily Griffith Beardsley Preserve
Delorme Connecticut/Rhode Island Atlas and Gazetteer: p. 32, E43; **Estimated GPS:** 41°34.61'N; 73°19.13'W
Views: Lateral, looking down and across from rim of gorge

Aesthetics: Fair/Good
Characteristics: Remote, scenic, small
Accessibility: 0.7 mile hike
Degree of Difficulty: Moderate
Information: Trail map available at www.roxburylandtrust.org /preserves.html

DESCRIPTION: The Caroline Glen Cascade, a series of small falls in a deep, narrow ravine, is on Moosehorn Brook—a small stream which rises north of Moosehorn Hill and flows into the Shepaug River north of Roxbury Station. A bench, strategically placed overlooking the ravine, provides a restful spot for quiet contemplation.

HISTORY: The waterfall and glen are located in the 121-acre Emily Griffith Beardsley Preserve which Caroline H. Beaumont, Elizabeth Boardman, and Hugh Hazelton, Jr., gave to the Roxbury Land Trust in 1976.

The glen was once a site of much activity when a sawmill operated downstream from the cascades. An impoundment created by the breached dam at the footbridge crossing brought water down to the mill through a sluiceway (still visible next to the pathway).

Troop 65 built the present footbridge in 1997 as an Eagle Scout project.

DIRECTIONS: From Roxbury (junction of CT 67 and CT 317) drive north on CT 67 for 0.8 mile. Bear right onto CT 199, and drive north for another 0.7 mile. Turn right at the sign for the preserve (immediately after house #157), and follow a dirt road for 50 feet to the parking area.

Walk around the metal barrier, and follow the blue-blazed loop trail east past private lands on your left. After 0.2 mile you will come to a kiosk and map of the preserve. A stone monument to your right commemorates the land donation made by the family of Hugh and Caroline Norton Hazelton.

Continue straight ahead on the main trail (an old mill road) for another 0.5 mile. Then turn left onto a blue-blazed spur trail, marked TO GLEN, that leads to the cascades and overlook in 100 feet. The dam and footbridge are just upstream from the overlook, where the trail follows a spine of land between the ravine and sluiceway.

17

See page 211 for hiking map

JACK'S BROOK CASCADE

Location: Roxbury (Litchfield County), Brian E. Tierney Preserve
Delorme Connecticut/Rhode Island Atlas and Gazetteer: p. 32, H4; **Estimated GPS:** 41°31.96'N; 73°17.41'W
Views: Head-on, lateral
Aesthetics: Good

Characteristics: Remote, scenic, small
Accessibility: 0.3-mile hike
Degree of Difficulty: Moderate
Information: Roxbury Land Trust, 860-350-4148; trail map: www.roxburylandtrust.org /preserves.html

DESCRIPTION: This pretty, 15-foot-high waterfall, known locally as the Cascades, is on Jack's Brook—a small stream which rises north of Booth Hill, and flows into the Shepaug River south of Roxbury. The waterfall is gently inclined, emerging from a deeply cut gorge. A sawmill once operated by the cascade, but little evidence remains of it today.

HISTORY: Jack's Brook Cascade is in the 56-acre Brian E. Tierney Preserve gifted to the Roxbury Land Trust by Dr. and Mrs. Robert Sherman in 1974 in memory of Brian E. Tierney, who was killed while fighting in Vietnam. The area by Jack's Brook at one time was heavily mined for sand and gravel.

DIRECTIONS: From Roxbury (junction of CT 317 and CT 67), drive southeast on CT 67 for 2.0 miles. Turn right onto Squire Road and proceed west for 0.5 mile. Pull into a small parking area on your left, just before reaching Apple Lane (which comes in on your right). The trail begins from the memorial plaque.

Follow the trail south for 0.1 mile, crossing two footbridges (the second was rebuilt in 1994 as a scout troop project). Immediately after crossing over Jack's Brook, turn left by the memorial stone and follow the blue-blazed trail upstream, heading southeast, for 0.2 mile to the cascade.

Upper part of Jack's Brook Cascade

ADDITIONAL CASCADE: Roxbury Falls, aka Shepaug Falls, is south of Roxbury in the tiny hamlet of Roxbury Falls. A series of small cascades (more like large rapids) can be seen both upstream and downstream from the Minor Bridge Road spanning the Shepaug River.

From Roxbury (junction of CT 67 and CT 317), go southwest on CT 67 for 0.2 mile, turn left, and then proceed south on South Street for roughly 3.0 miles. Turn right onto Minor Bridge Road, and drive 0.3 mile to the bridge. No parking signs abound, meaning that you must now find a place to park elsewhere and walk back. Although Sherman Park is directly next to the bridge, you are not allowed in there unless you are a resident of Roxbury Falls.

18

SAUGATUCK FALLS NATURAL AREA

Location: Northwest of Diamond Hill (Fairfield County), Saugatuck Falls Natural Area
Delorme Connecticut/Rhode Island Atlas and Gazetteer: p. 22, 19; **Estimated GPS:** 41°18.32'N; 73°24.20'W
Views: Head-on
Aesthetics: Good

Characteristics: Remote, historic, scenic, small
Accessibility: 1.0-mile hike
Degree of Difficulty: Moderately difficult
Information: Information (no trail map) available at www.berkshirehiking.com/hikes/saugatuck_falls.html

DESCRIPTION: The falls contained at the Saugatuck Falls Natural Area are on the Saugatuck River—a 25-mile-long stream which rises from Watoba Lake southwest of Danbury and flows into Long Island Sound southeast of Norwalk. The main cascade is 6 feet high and located directly upstream from a right-angle turn in the river. Several smaller cascades are formed just upstream from the main cascade, where old mill foundations reveal a history of past industrialization. Take note, however, that this part of the stream is on land posted by the Public Water Supply.

Falls Hole is the name of the pool at the base of the main falls formed, in part, by huge flat slabs of rock that enable hikers to rock hop across the river.

HISTORY: The creation of the Saugatuck Falls Natural Area in 1968 was a cooperative effort between Redding, the State of Connecticut, and the U.S. Department of Housing and Urban Development.

Saugatuck is a corruption of the Native American word *sauki-tuk,* meaning "outlet of tidal river" or "river that flows out," a word that makes sense when you apply it to the village of Saugatuck located further south at the mouth of the Saugatuck River.

The natural area contains over 312 acres of land with 5 miles of trails.

DIRECTIONS: From southeast of Danbury (junction of CT 53 and CT 302) drive south on CT 53 for 5.7 miles and turn right into a small pull-out opposite John Read Middle School.

From south of Redding (junction of CT 107 and CT 53) go northwest on CT 53 (Redding Road) for 0.8 mile. Look for the tiny parking area to your left, opposite John Read Middle School. If no space is available in front of the park entrance, drive into the school and park off to the side.

The trail starts from between two large stone pillars. In less than 0.1 mile you will cross a footbridge (replaced in March of 2012) that spans a ponded section of the Saugatuck River. After another several hundred feet turn right off the main trail onto a white-blazed path labeled FALLS TRAIL. You will quickly pass through a meadow and then down the base of a rocky hill that leads you to the Saugatuck River.

Continue following the white-blazed trail, which now parallels the west bank of the Saugatuck River, heading upstream. The sounds of CT 53 will be clearly audible across the river. Sections of this path may be challenging because of rocky footing. In roughly 1.0 mile you will come to the falls. The best views are from the white-blazed trail along the west bank.

ADDITIONAL CASCADES: Several roadside waterfalls can be seen on nearby Aspetuck River (a different Aspetuck River from the one described in the entry on Aspetuck Falls in New Preston).

From southwest of Redding (junction of CT 53 and CT 107), drive northeast on CT 107 (Hill Road) for 0.9 mile. Bear right onto Cross Highway and continue northeast for nearly 2.0 miles. When you come to CT 58 continue straight ahead, now on Church Hill Road, for another 0.5 mile. Then turn right onto Poverty Hollow Road and head south for over 0.3 mile. Cross over a one-lane bridge (where the falls are), drive 0.05 mile farther, and park in a small pullout on your left—the site of an old mill (41°18.69'N; 73°20.11'W). Walk back up to the one-lane bridge for views of the gorge and falls. A particularly attractive waterfall is directly beneath the bridge.

Pay strict attention to traffic, for the road is narrow and little room has been set aside for pedestrians.

19

SHEEP FALLS

Location: South of Georgetown (Fairfield County), Town Forest Park
Delorme Connecticut/Rhode Island Atlas and Gazetteer: p. 19, A19; **Estimated GPS:** 41°14.63'N; 73°26.71'W

Views: Head-on
Aesthetics: Fair/Good
Characteristics: Remote, scenic, small
Accessibility: 0.2-mile walk
Degree of Difficulty: Moderately easy

DESCRIPTION: Sheep Falls is on Barretts Brook, a small stream which rises from hills west of Georgetown and flows into Streets Pond.

The waterfall is no higher than 3 feet, but surrounded by exposed bedrock and located in a setting that is bucolic and peaceful. Sheep Falls is the perfect example of why one can't rush to judgment about the attractiveness of a waterfall based merely on its size.

Just downstream from the falls along the east bank is a large, flat boulder that provides a wonderful surface to sit on while enjoying views of the waterfall. It is also a great place to enjoy a bite of food.

HISTORY: Sheep Falls' name is a throwback to a time when sheep would be brought down to the stream to drink.

Georgetown is at the convergence of Wilton, Redding, and Weston. It's a village that came into its own with the establishment of the Gilbert and Bennett Manufacturing Company, manufacturers of iron wire, wire cloth, sieves, and cheese and meat safes.

DIRECTIONS: From Georgetown (junction of CT 107, US 7, and Mountain Road) turn west onto Mountain Road and proceed south, heading uphill for 0.7 mile. When you come to Indian Hill Road, turn right and head west for 0.05 mile. Then turn left onto Pin Oak Road and drive south for 0.3 mile until you come to a cul-de-sac.

From the cul-de-sac, walk south on a driveway heading toward a private residence. In 30 feet you will reach the trailhead to your right. Follow the path for 0.05 mile until you come to a junction. Bear right, proceeding downhill for several hundred feet until you reach Barretts Brook. Instead of crossing over the stream via two footbridges, turn left onto a blue-blazed trail. After 0.05 mile, bear right onto an orange-blazed path that leads quickly to Barretts Brook and the waterfall.

20

AMBLER CASCADE

Location: Northwest of Weston (Fairfield County), Lucius Pond Ordway Devil's Den Preserve
Delorme Connecticut/Rhode Island Atlas and Gazetteer: p. 19, A21; **Estimated GPS:** 41°14.19'N; 73°23.81'W
Views: Head-on
Aesthetics: Fair
Characteristics: Remote, scenic, small
Accessibility: 1.2-mile hike

Degree of Difficulty: Moderate
Information: Lucius Pond Ordway Devil's Den Preserve, 860-344-0716; trail map available at www.nature.org/ourinitiatives /regions/northamerica/unitedstates /connecticut/placesweprotect/devils -den-trail-mappdf.null
Hours: Daily, sunrise to sunset from spring through fall; gates are locked at sunset

DESCRIPTION: Ambler Cascade, aka Amber Cascade, is a 3-foot-high cascade on a tiny tributary to the west branch of the Saugatuck River. The accumulation of boulders that have fallen into the ravine distinguish this cascade. It is through this rock-choked gorge that the stream makes its way over and around large boulders, producing tiny cascades in the process. It is a very scenic, natural area.

A footbridge crosses the stream at the foot of the gorge. Directly below the bridge a small cascade tumbles into a pool of water.

HISTORY: Ambler Cascade is in the Lucius Pond Ordway Devil's Den Preserve, a 1,746-acre sanctuary owned by the Nature Conservancy. The preserve contains 20 miles of interlocking trails, and is the largest nature preserve in southwestern Connecticut. The park was created in 1966 through the generosity of Katherine Ordway, whose donation enabled The Nature Conservancy to purchase 1,400 acres of land.

Imprints in the bedrock—naturally formed potholes—led to the name Devil's Den by early settlers, particularly those with vivid imaginations, who saw the cloven hoofprints of the devil in the rock. Locals refer to the preserve simply as "The Den."

Archaeological evidence shows that the Devil's Den was used by Native Americans as far back as five thousand years ago. The overhanging rock ledges served as excellent shelters while hunting. Later, from the 1800s to about 1920, the den was a major site for charcoal production, where up to 30 kilns operated.

The Devil is popular in Connecticut and for good reason. Over 34 sites specifically mention him either by name or nickname. Five of these are Devil's Dens, the other four being located in Plainfield, Monroe, Franklin, and Sterling. Four are Devil's Backbones, two are Devil's Footprints, two are Devil's Rocks, and two are Devil's Kitchens. By any manner of reckoning, the Devil is no stranger to Connecticut!

Surprisingly the name of the cascade does not refer to the way hikers may "amble" through the glen, but rather it is a memorial to generations of the Ambler-Raymond family, who lived in the area from 1802 to 1979.

DIRECTIONS: From northwest of Weston (junction of CT 57 and CT 53) head northwest on CT 57 for 1.3 miles. Turn right on Godfrey Road and drive northeast for 0.6 mile. Then turn left on Pent Road and head northwest for over 0.3 mile into the parking area for the preserve.

From this point on, it is best to have a trail guide in your hand, which can be picked up from the kiosk at the parking lot. Essentially, the hike takes you along the Pent Trail, a nondrivable continuation of Pent Road, for about 1.0 mile and then left onto the Ambler Trail, which leads into the gorge after 0.2 mile.

ADDITIONAL CASCADE: A 5-foot-high roadside cascade, called Valley Forge Falls by some locals, is in a pretty flume on the Saugatuck River. From Weston (junction of CT 57 and CT 53), drive southeast on CT 57 for 3.6 miles. Turn left onto Lyons Plain Road and head north for 3.7 miles. When you come to a fork where Kelloggs Hill Road goes right, veer left onto Valley Forge Road, ignore the immediate left-hand turn for David Hill Road, and proceed north for 1.6 miles. You will come to a small bridge with views of the cascade (41°14.69'N; 73°20.94'W).

Additional cascades can be seen roughly 0.05–0.1 mile further downstream.

FALLS ACCESSIBLE FROM CT 8

CT 8 enters Connecticut from Massachusetts, initially following the west branch of the Farmington River until it begins to slowly veer away after reaching the south end of Colebrook River Lake. From here CT 8 parallels the Still River, passes through Winsted, which lies in a pocket created by the Still River and Mad River, and comes to Torrington, a high hill town deeply cut by various branches of the Naugatuck River. At this point CT

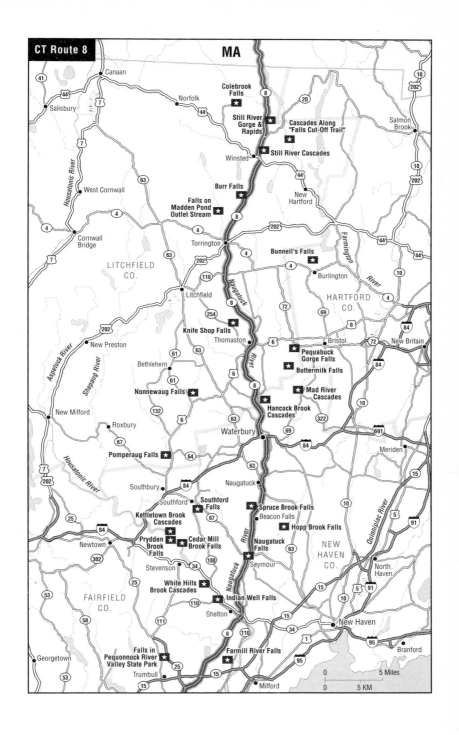

CT Route 8

MA

Canaan
41
44
Salisbury
7

Norfolk
44

Colebrook
Falls ⭐
8
20
10
202

Still River
Gorge &
Rapids ⭐

Cascades Along
"Falls Cut-Off Trail" ⭐

Salmon
Brook

Winsted
Still River Cascades ⭐

10
202

Housatonic River
West Cornwall
63

44
New
Hartford

Burr Falls ⭐

Falls on
Madden Pond
Outlet Stream ⭐
8

4
Cornwall
Bridge
7
4
4

Torrington
202
202
4

Bunnell's Falls ⭐
4
Burlington

Farmington River
44
44

10
4

LITCHFIELD
CO.
63
118

HARTFORD
CO.

Naugatuck
Litchfield
8
254
72
69
6
84

Knife Shop Falls ⭐
Thomaston
6
Bristol
72
New Britain

New Preston
202
61
63

Pequabuck
Gorge Falls ⭐
Buttermilk Falls ⭐
84

Aspetuck River
Shepaug River
Bethlehem
61
6

Nonnewaug Falls ⭐
132
River
8
Mad River
Cascades ⭐
10

New Milford
Roxbury
67
6
63
Hancock Brook
Cascades ⭐
322

Waterbury
69
I-84

Pomperaug Falls ⭐
64
63
Meriden

Housatonic River
7
202
84

Southbury
Naugatuck
63
691
15

Southford
Falls ⭐
Southford
Kettletown Brook
Cascades ⭐
67
Spruce Brook Falls ⭐
Beacon Falls
Hopp Brook Falls ⭐
10
Quinnipiac River
91

25
84
Newtown
Prydden
Brook
Falls ⭐
Cedar Mill
Brook Falls ⭐
Naugatuck
Falls ⭐
63
NEW
HAVEN
CO.
North
Haven
5
91

302
Stevenson
34
188
Seymour
15

53
White Hills
Brook Cascades ⭐
5
91

FAIRFIELD
CO.
25
110
Indian Well Falls ⭐
10
15

58
111
Shelton
15
New Haven

34
1
95
Branford

Georgetown
Falls in
Pequonnock River
Valley State Park ⭐
Farmill River Falls ⭐
95

25
Trumbull
15
Milford

53
15

0   5 Miles
0   5 KM

8 switches allegiance to the Naugatuck River and heads south to Seymour, where it begins following the Housatonic River to Derby—a medium-sized village at the head of tidewater on the Housatonic—where it joins the Naugatuck River. From here CT 8 heads southwest, gradually pulling away from the Housatonic River, until it finally comes to an end at I-95 in Bridgeport by Long Island Sound.

There are a number of significant routes that branch off from CT 8 to both the east and west, and a number have waterfall-bearing streams. At Winsted, US 44 heads northwest to Norfolk and southeast to New Hartford. At Torrington, US 202 goes southwest toward Litchfield, and east toward Canton and Collinsville. At Thomaston, US 6 proceeds southwest toward Watertown, and east toward Bristol. At Waterbury, I-84 goes southwest toward Southbury, and east toward Marion. At Shelton, CT 110 proceeds west toward Monroe, and south toward Stratford.

21

COLEBROOK FALLS

Location: Colebrook (Litchfield County)
Delorme Connecticut/Rhode Island Atlas and Gazetteer: p. 51, D16; **Estimated GPS:** 41°59.49'N; 73°05.86'W

Views: Above, distant; lateral, distant
Aesthetics: Fair
Characteristics: Remote, historic, small
Accessibility: Roadside

DESCRIPTION: Colebrook Falls is a 10-foot-high, terraced cascade on Center Brook, a small stream which rises west of Colebrook and flows into Sandy Brook northeast of Colebrook. Extensive foundation ruins are evident along the north bank near the base of the cascade.

HISTORY: At one time the marshlands west of CT 183 were dammed up and the impoundment used to furnish waterpower to a tannery and two forges at Colebrook Center. The Rockwell brothers—Solomon, Reuben, Alpha, and Martin—operated one of the forges. Problems were created by the impoundment as time went on, however. A fever swept through the community and was thought to be created by the extensive shallow-water pond. The dam was lowered and the pond drained to disinfect the atmos-

Colebrook Falls—fallen into relative obscurity over the years (the image on the left is of a ca. 1910 postcard; the image on the right of a 2012 photograph)

phere. As a result of this action, factories dependent upon the stream for waterpower were forced to relocate to more suitable areas.

Colebrook was earlier spelled Coldbrook, no doubt a reference to the frigidity of its springtime waters.

DIRECTIONS: From Colebrook (junction of CT 183 and CT 182A) drive north on CT 183 (Colebrook Road) for 0.2 mile. You will cross over Center Brook. The falls are directly downstream to your right. It is possible to obtain views looking over the top of the cascade from the bridge, but these are less than satisfactory.

A hundred feet north on CT 183, to your right, is the Colebrook Center Cemetery with distant, lateral views of the cascade when the trees are bereft of leaves.

There are also partial views from Center Brook Road just south of the bridge, but these are limited due to intervening houses.

22

STILL RIVER GORGE AND RAPIDS

Location: Robertsville (Litchfield County)
Delorme Connecticut/Rhode Island Atlas and Gazetteer: p. 51, E19; **Estimated GPS:** 41°58.17'N; 73°02.37'W

Views: Head-on, lateral
Aesthetics: Fair
Characteristics: Rural, small
Accessibility: Roadside

DESCRIPTION: These tiny cascades are formed on the Still River, a medium-sized stream which rises north of Torrington and flows into the west branch of the Farmington River at Riverton. What makes this area so appealing is the impressive gorge. It is impossible not to be caught up in the sights and sounds of the river as it comes roaring by.

HISTORY: A short distance further downstream at the confluence of Sandy Brook and the Still River are the foundation ruins of the Richard Smith iron furnace which operated from 1770 to 1810 in what was then called Old Forge.

Sandy Brook was originally spelled Sandys Brook after Samuel Sandys of Boston.

DIRECTIONS: From Robertsville (junction of Riverton Road and CT 8), turn east onto Riverton Road and proceed southeast for 0.6 mile.

When you come to Old Forge Road, turn right, immediately crossing over a stone bridge which spans Sandy Brook. After 0.2 mile turn left onto Creamery Road and in 0.05 mile you will come to a bridge spanning the Still River at the intersection of Creamery Road and Ruth Cross Road. Park in a tiny pullout at the southeast end of the bridge.

From Nelson Corner (junction of CT 20 and CT 8), drive north on CT 8 for 1.4 miles. Turn right onto Robertsville Road and drive northeast for 0.5 mile. At the junction with Old Forge Road, on your left, continue straight ahead on what is now Creamery Road for less than 0.05 mile further, crossing over the Still River. Park to your right at the end of the bridge.

The upper part of the gorge can be seen from the top of the bridge. There are a number of small cascades and rapids but none are distinctive enough to be singled out. More cascades are visible downstream. Within a

Tunxis Falls, near Winsted, Conn.

Tunxis Falls—pretty, but posted (ca. 1910 postcard)

The Still River—anything but still

couple of hundred feet the river reaches a narrow, chiseled gorge where additional rapids and tiny cascades abound.

To visit the confluence of the Still River and Sandy Brook, drive back the way you came to the south end of the bridge by Riverton Road. Roughly 150 feet from the bridge are old foundation ruins, not far from the confluence of the Still River and Sandy Brook. The lower gorge on the Still River is several hundred feet upstream from here.

ADDITIONAL CASCADE: Roughly 0.3 mile further upstream on the Still River is spectacular Tunxis Falls—a dammed waterfall of substantial size in a narrow gorge. The waterfall generates hydroelectric power via a power plant stationed on the west bank of the gorge by the falls for Northeast Utilities. The area unfortunately is posted and off-limits to the public.

Tunxis is a Native American word for "place of turning," an apt description of the Still River and its myriad of turns as it makes its way towards the Farmington River.

23

CASCADES ALONG FALLS CUT OFF TRAIL

Location: Northwest of New Hartford (Litchfield County), Peoples State Forest
Delorme Connecticut/Rhode Island Atlas and Gazetteer: p. 51, G21; **Estimated GPS:** 41°56.60'N; 73°00.48'W
Views: Lateral
Aesthetics: Fair

Characteristics: Remote, seasonal
Accessibility: 0.1-mile hike
Degree of Difficulty: Moderately difficult
Information: Peoples State Forest, 860-379-2469; trail map www.ct.gov/dep/lib/dep/stateparks/maps/peoples.pdf

DESCRIPTION: Two unnamed, seasonal cascades have formed on a tiny stream running down into the west branch of the Farmington River from the river's mountainous east side. Both cascades are fairly undefined, but are definitely more than just steeply cascading streams. The lowermost cascade is 40 to 50 feet high but difficult to see as a whole because of its path through a field of enormous boulders. The upper cascade is farther up the mountainside, out of range of the talus field but still broken up into parts.

Exactly 299 strategically placed rock steps facilitate the climb up to the cascades—an ascent which should not be attempted when ice overlays the trail. This seasonal cascade also has a limited watershed. Only visit in early spring or after heavy, prolonged rainfall.

HISTORY: The cascades are located in the Peoples State Forest—a nature preserve covering nearly 3,000 acres with over 11 miles of hiking trails that was established in 1924 through the combined efforts of private individuals, citizen groups like the Daughters of the American Revolution and the Connecticut Federation of Women's Clubs, and nonprofits like the Connecticut Forest and Park Association. The trails are named after key individuals who played a role in creating the preserve, a clear break from what up until then had been a tradition of using only Native American names.

The concept of establishing a state forest through private donations originated with Alain White of Litchfield and Mrs. Franklin W. Gerard (informally known as Jessie Gerard) of New Haven. Each eight dollars donated enabled one acre of land to be purchased. Gerard was heavily involved with the Connecticut Federation of Women's Clubs. She was so well thought of that the club donated 37 acres of forest in her memory.

The trailhead begins at the Barkhamsted Lighthouse, a site whose name has a humorous origin, and nothing to do with an actual lighthouse. A young white woman named Molly Barber from Wethersfield spited her father by eloping with a Narragansett Indian named James Chaugham (pronounced "Shawn") and settled into a cabin at the spot currently occupied by the parking area. Stagecoach drivers, seeing the light in the cabin at night as they drove by, would yell out "There's the Barkhamsted Lighthouse! Only five more miles to New Hartford!" In time the area became an outcast village for African Americans, Native Americans, and wayward whites just as it did at Satan's Kingdom in New Hartford.

DIRECTIONS: From northwest of New Harford (junction of US 44 and CT 181), drive north on CT 181 (River Road) for 1.4 miles. Turn right onto CT 318 (Saville Dam Road) and head east for 0.1 mile, crossing over the Farmington River bridge. Turn left onto East River Road.

From Barkhamsted (junction of CT 179 and CT 219), head southwest on CT 219 (East Hartland Road) for 2.5 miles. Just east of the Saville Dam, located at the south end of the Barkhamsted Reservoir, turn right onto CT 318 and proceed west for 2.4 miles. Then turn right onto East River Road before crossing over a bridge spanning the west branch of the Farmington River.

Coming from either direction, head north on East River Road for 2.4 miles. Pull into the parking area on your left, directly overlooking the river. The trailhead begins on the opposite side of the road.

Begin following the blue/yellow-blazed Jessie Gerard Trail uphill. In less than 100 feet bear left, switching to the blue/red-blazed Falls Cut Off Trail. Follow this trail steadily uphill, heading essentially north. In less than 0.1 mile you will reach a huge talus slope of large boulders, many the sizes of automobiles, where the stream weaves its way down steeply between the rocks and across slides of bedrock. Continue climbing up the Falls Cut Off Trail with the talus field to your left. Be prepared for a fairly steep climb. Within a hundred feet, you will have views of a 40- to 50-foot-high cascade broken up into sections by the talus. If you continue uphill several hundred feet higher you will reach a point where a 20-foot-high cascade can be seen.

24

STILL RIVER CASCADES

Location: Winsted (Litchfield County)
Delorme Connecticut/Rhode Island Atlas and Gazetteer: p. 51, H18; **Estimated GPS:** 41°55.83'N; 73°03.48'W

Views: Head-on
Aesthetics: Fair
Characteristics: Urban, historic, small
Accessibility: Roadside

DESCRIPTION: The cascades in Winsted are formed on the Still River, a medium-sized stream which rises north of Torrington and flows into the west branch of the Farmington River at Riverton. The Still River is anything but still, however, as it races through Winsted with considerable authority.

The upper cascade is over 6 feet high, divided in the middle by an upraised section of bedrock. An old stone wall is evident along the west bank, perhaps from an abandoned road. On the east bank is an old bridge abutment.

Downstream from the Wallens Street Bridge is a smaller cascade next to the former Gilbert Clock Company, whose building now serves as an apartment complex.

HISTORY: Winsted was settled in 1756, becoming one of the first mill towns in the state.

The Gilbert Clock Shop Apartments is the surviving section of a complex of buildings that once constituted the William L. Gilbert Clock Company, at one time one of the largest clock-makers in the world. Originally a gristmill built by Elias Balcomb in 1776 occupied the site. The clock factory employed 500 workers and produced two thousand clocks per day. It was converted into an apartment building in the 1980s.

DIRECTIONS: From the center of Winsted (junction of CT 8 and US 44/CT 183), proceed north on CT 8 for 0.6 mile until you come to a traffic light.

From Nelson Corner (junction of CT 20 and CT 8), drive south on CT 8 for 1.2 miles until you come to a traffic light.

Approaching from either direction, turn east onto Wallens Street, immediately crossing over the Still River. Park near the Gilbert Clock Shop Apartments or at Still River Commons. Walk back to the Wallens Street Bridge for upstream and downstream views of the cascades.

ADDITIONAL CASCADE #1: Driving south from Winsted on the Winsted/Torrington Road (initially called Rowley Street), turn right onto a secondary road at 1.3 miles. Within 50 feet you will come to a 15-foot-high seasonal cascade (41°54.26'N; 73°04.16'W). This unnamed cascade is on a tiny tributary to the Still River which rises from a swampy area atop the mountainous ridge.

Several small falls by the former Gilbert Clock Company on the Still River

ADDITIONAL CASCADE #2: From New Winsted (junction of US 44 and CT 8) drive southeast on US 44 for over 8.0 miles and turn left into the entrance for Satan's Kingdom State Recreation Park just before reaching the US 44 bridge which spans the Farmington River. Proceed south on Satan's Kingdom Park Road to its end (41°51.34'N; 72°57.45'W) and park. Continuing on foot, follow the yellow-blazed trail downriver through a deep gorge for 0.1 mile until you come to a narrow, 30-foot-high, seasonal cascade that drops vertically down the east wall.

ADDITIONAL CASCADE #3: Before leaving Nelson Corner to see the Still River Cascades, be sure to take a quick look at a 20-foot-high cascade located on the west side of the road next to a private residence, virtually at the junction of CT 8, CT 20, and Smith Hill Road (41°56.81'N; 73°03.03'W).

25

BURR FALLS

Location: Burrville (Litchfield County)

Delorme Connecticut/Rhode Island Atlas and Gazetteer: p. 51, K16; **Estimated GPS:** 41°52.16'N; 73°05.20'W

Views: Head-on, lateral

Aesthetics: Good

Characteristics: Rural, historic, medium-sized

Accessibility: Roadside for Burr Falls, several hundred foot bushwhack to lower cascades

Degree of Difficulty: Moderate

Information: Burr Pond State Park, 860-482-1817

DESCRIPTION: Burr Falls is a 40-foot-high cascade on the outlet stream from 0.7-mile-long Burr Pond. Just below Burr Falls are the stone-block ruins of the Borden factory.

Several hundred feet upstream from Burr Falls is a 10-foot-high elongated cascade. A hundred feet downstream from Burr Falls are two smaller cascades. The first is 12 feet high with a stone-block dam across its top. The second, lower cascade is 8 feet in height and block-shaped. Remnants of a breached stone dam can be seen at its top.

HISTORY: Burr Falls is named after Milo Burr, who dammed up the outlet stream from Burr Pond in 1851. His house can be seen directly across the road from the ruins of the Borden factory.

Burr Falls, a roadside waterfall with history

Near the base of Burr Falls are the foundation ruins of Gail Borden's condensed milk factory, the first of its kind in the world. You may not remember the ad, particularly if you're under 50, but "If it's Borden's, it's got to be good" was a household phrase for many years. Borden established his condensed milk plant in 1857. Fire destroyed the factory in 1877.

Borden's process for creating condensed milk involved heating up the milk to the boiling point to sterilize it, killing all the bacteria present. Then 75 percent of the milk's content was allowed to evaporate, with sugar, a preservative, added to the remainder. The first milk product produced by Borden was named "Eagle Brand."

It is said that Borden's process of preserving milk through evaporation and condensation proved of enormous benefit to the Union Army during the Civil War, for it provided them with a means for taking along nourishment without spoilage.

In addition to Borden's plant, a tannery and three sawmills also used the outlet stream for hydropower.

Just a short distance upstream from Burr Falls is 436-acre Burr Pond State Park.

DIRECTIONS: From Winsted (junction of US 44 and CT 8) proceed south on CT 8 for about 3.0 miles. Get off at exit 46, and proceed west on Highland Lake Road for 0.2 mile. When you come to Winsted/Torrington Road, turn left and drive south for 1.0 mile to reach Burrville.

Approaching from Torrington on CT 8, get off at exit 45. Turn left onto Kennedy Drive and proceed west for 0.1 mile. Then turn right onto Winsted/Torrington Road and head north for 2.8 miles to Burrville.

Coming from either direction turn west onto Burr Mountain Road and drive northwest, heading steeply uphill, for 0.2 mile. Parking is at a tiny pullout large enough to accommodate one car on your left, just past the historic sign for the Borden factory. If the space is already taken, drive uphill for another 0.1 mile and park next to the Burr Pond State Park access gate, making sure not to block it. From here it is but a 0.1-mile walk down the road to roadside views of Burr Falls and the Borden factory ruins.

26

FALLS ON MADDEN POND OUTLET STREAM

Location: North of Torrington (Litchfield County), Sunnybrook State Park
Delorme Connecticut/Rhode Island Atlas and Gazetteer: p. 42, A2; **Estimated GPS:** 41°51.06'N; 73°07.57'W
Views: Head-on, lateral
Aesthetics: Fair/Good
Characteristics: Remote, scenic, small
Accessibility: 0.2-mile walk

Degree of Difficulty: Moderately easy (except for 100-foot bushwhack if you wish to reach the base of cascade)
Information: Trail map available in Ann T. Colson (ed.), *Connecticut Walk Book: The Guide to the Blue-Blazed Hiking Trails of Western Connecticut* (19th ed.), (Connecticut Forest & Park Association, 2006), page 283.

DESCRIPTION: Several cascades have formed on the outlet creek from Madden Pond, a tiny stream which flows into the east branch of the Naugatuck River.

The main waterfall—a 5-foot-high, block-shaped cascade—drops into a small pool. Just upstream are two smaller drops. Downstream from a footbridge is a tiny, 3-foot-high fall. The cascades are surrounded by a landscape of enormous boulders.

HISTORY: The Alain and May White Nature Trails, which include the Madden Pond tract, are part of more than 6,000 acres of land donated by Alain White and his sister, May. Alain White also notably served as president of the Connecticut Forest & Park Association from 1923 to 1928.

The trails at Sunnybrook State Park were developed by Jerome and Lorrie Bacca in the early 1980s. The park now encompasses 464 acres of land.

DIRECTIONS: From Torrington (junction of CT 4 and CT 8) drive southwest on CT 4 (East Elm Street) for 0.5 mile. Turn right onto North Main Street and drive north for 0.5 mile. At a fork, bear left onto Newfield Road (continuing to parallel the east branch of the Naugatuck River, to your left) and proceed north for over 2.3 miles. Sunnybrook State Park is on your left, the entrance marked by two stone pillars.

From the parking area, walk past the yellow barricade and head south along the main road (now a pedestrian walk) for 0.1 mile. Before crossing over a bridge that spans the east branch of the Naugatuck River, turn right onto a blue-blazed trail and head west for 0.1 mile. You will come to a foot-bridge which crosses over the Madden Pond outlet stream. If you look upstream you will see the main cascade, roughly 100 feet away (which can be easily bushwhacked up to).

If you continue bushwhacking past the cascade, you will observe that the stream has a dikelike look to it, as though someone had bulldozed earth and rocks up to the bank of the stream in order to create a long retaining wall.

By crossing over the footbridge and immediately turning left onto a yellow-blazed trail, you will come to a 3-foot cascade just downstream from the footbridge.

27

KNIFE SHOP FALLS

Location: Northfield (Litchfield County), Humaston Brook State Park
Delorme Connecticut/Rhode Island Atlas and Gazetteer: p. 42, J3; **Estimated GPS:** 41°41.95'N; 73°06.18'W
Views: Head-on, lateral
Aesthetics: Excellent

Characteristics: Rural, historic, scenic, medium-sized
Accessibility: 100-foot walk to views of first and second cascade; roadside views of third cascade
Degree of Difficulty: First two cascades—easy; third cascade—moderately difficult if bushwhacking to it

DESCRIPTION: Knife Shop Falls consists of three attractive cascades formed on Humaston Brook, a small stream which rises from the hills north of Northfield and flows into the Naugatuck River in Thomaston.

The first and second cascades are 15 feet high and separated by less than 100 feet. What's deceptive is how the stream turns dramatically between the two cascades, initially making the second cascade appear to be formed on a tributary to Humaston Brook. The third cascade is 50 feet downstream from the upper two. It is 10 feet high, with a pool at its base. Above it is a slide cascade. Foundation ruins abound by all three cascades.

One of three pretty waterfalls that have formed on Humaston Brook within a span of several hundred feet

HISTORY: Built in 1854, the Knife Shop Dam, less than 0.1 mile upstream from the three cascades, impounded Humaston Brook to create a small lake for hydropower. The dam was restored in 1983.

In 1853 a series of buildings were constructed at the falls by 20 men from Northfield to manufacture wagons, sleighs, carriages, clothespins, and a variety of wooden novelties. After five years the Northfield Knife Company bought the property and used the shops to produce pocket cutlery. A series of line shafts, belts, and pulleys transferred power from a waterwheel to the machinery.

In 1926 the State of Connecticut acquired the property and it became part of the 141-acre Humaston Brook State Park.

DIRECTIONS: From Thomaston (junction of CT 254 and US 6) drive northwest on CT 254 for 2.6 miles. Turn right at a traffic light onto Knife Shop Road (a loop road whose south end was passed at 2.1 miles), and proceed northeast for less than 0.2 mile. Then turn left onto Newton Road and park on the left side of the road near the dam.

From where you parked, walk south down Knife Shop Road for less than 100 feet. A pathway to your right leads over to the gorge where you can see the first and second cascades, as well as numerous factory ruins. There is no path to the third, lowermost cascade.

28

BUNNELL'S FALLS

Location: North of Burlington (Hartford County)
Delorme Connecticut/Rhode Island Atlas and Gazetteer: p. 42, E11; **Estimated GPS:** 41°47.11'N; 72°57.99'W

Views: Lateral, from side of gorge looking upstream
Aesthetics: Good
Characteristics: Rural, historic, medium-sized
Accessibility: 0.05-mile walk
Degree of Difficulty: Easy

DESCRIPTION: Bunnell's Falls is a 15-foot-high waterfall on Burlington Brook, aka Bunnell Brook, which rises west of Burlington and flows into the Farmington River northeast of Burlington. The stream and waterfall are likely named after Joel Bunnell, or possibly a close family member.

HISTORY: Near the falls are the foundation ruins of the Hotchkiss Watch Factory established by Elisha Hotchkiss, which manufactured both clock casings and movements. The factory failed in the mid-1830s.

DIRECTIONS: From Burlington (junction of CT 4 and CT 69) proceed east on CT 4 (Spielman Highway) for 0.5 mile and turn left onto Covey Road.

From Collinsville (west end of the CT 179 bridge spanning the Farmington River), drive south on CT 179 (Canton Road) for 2.0 miles. When you come to CT 4 (Spielman Highway) turn right and proceed southwest for 2.3 miles until you reach Covey Road, on your right.

Approaching from either direction, head north on Covey Road for 1.0 mile. Then turn right onto Hotchkiss Road and drive northeast for 0.2 mile. Pull off the road next to the foundation ruins of the Hotchkiss Watch Factory on your right.

Follow a path that goes between the watch factory ruins over to Burlington Brook, and then proceed left along the top of the gorge for lateral views of the falls. You will walk through what appears to be an abandoned sluiceway—an artificially dug channel to carry water—that

During earlier years, the Hotchkiss Watch Factory overlooked Bunnell's Falls.

comes to an end after several hundred feet. Look further downstream to see more foundation ruins along the north side of the bank.

ADDITIONAL CASCADE: At 0.2 mile further downstream next to Hotchkiss Road, opposite two wide pullouts, is a second waterfall, possibly called Vineyard Falls (41°47.19'N; 72°57.85'W). Although posted by the New Britain Water Department and therefore not directly accessible, the falls can be seen from Hotchkiss Road, albeit from a distance looking upstream, if you walk several hundred feet down from the pullouts to where the road veers to the right.

29

BUTTERMILK FALLS

Location: Tolles (Litchfield
County), Hancock Brook Park
**Delorme Connecticut/Rhode
Island Atlas and Gazetteer:**
p. 33, A21; **Estimated GPS:**
41°38.68'N; 73°00.43'W
Views: Head-on, lateral
Aesthetics: Excellent
Characteristics: Remote, scenic,
large, tall
Accessibility: 0.05- to 0.1-mile
hike

Degree of Difficulty: Overlook
of falls—easy; to base of falls—
moderate; upper cascades—
moderately easy
Information: Trail map available in
Ann T. Colson (ed.), *Connecticut
Walk Book: The Guide to the Blue-
Blazed Hiking Trails of Western
Connecticut* (19th ed.), (Connecticut
Forest & Park Association, 2006),
page 134.

DESCRIPTION: Buttermilk Falls is a terraced 60-foot-high cascade on
Hancock Brook, a medium-sized stream which rises from a tiny pond east
of Fall Mountain and flows into the Naugatuck River south of Waterville.
Two small cascades are encountered just above the top of the waterfall.

Several more cascades have formed 0.05 mile further upstream and can
be reached by following the blue-blazed path as it leads through a veritable
rock garden of large boulders.

HISTORY: Buttermilk Falls is in Hancock Brook Park, a tiny preserve
owned and managed by the Nature Conservancy.

The 36-mile-long Mattatuck Trail leads past the waterfall as it makes its
way distantly between Wolcott and the Mohawk Mountain State Park ski
area.

DIRECTIONS: From CT 8 get off at exit 39 for Bristol and Thomaston. Take US 6 east for 2.8 miles to Terryville. Turn right onto Eagle Street
and go south for 2.5 miles. When you come out to South Main Street (a
main highway), turn left and then immediately right onto Lane Hill Road.
Proceed steeply uphill for less than 0.2 mile. Look for a small pullout on
your right which is only large enough for two cars. Parking is also available
at the bottom of Lane Hill on the west side of South Main Street. Take
note that Lane Hill Road is closed during the winter.

From the parking space, follow the blue-blazed trail immediately across

Buttermilk Falls, one of Connecticut's highest waterfalls

Pequabuck Gorge Falls

a footbridge spanning a dry ravine and then directly over to a superb over-look of Buttermilk Falls. A secondary path leads steeply down to the base of the falls, but it is not necessary to scramble down this path in order to appreciate this waterfall.

The blue-blazed Mattatuck Trail follows upstream along the north bank of the brook, leading you up and around the top of the falls and then past several smaller cascades over the next 0.05 mile.

ADDITIONAL CASCADE: Pequabuck Gorge Falls, aka Plymouth Water Control Falls, is a partially dammed cascade on the Pequabuck River. From east of Terryville (junction of US 6 and CT 72), drive southeast on CT 72 for 1.0 mile, turn right onto Canal Street, and drive west for nearly 0.2 mile until you come to the Ted Knight Bridge where there are upstream (east) views of the tiny gorge and cascade (41°40.17'N; 72°59.62'W).

30

See page 211 for hiking map

NONNEWAUG FALLS

Location: Bethlehem (Litchfield County), Leever-Nonnewaug Falls Preserve
Delorme Connecticut/Rhode Island Atlas and Gazetteer: p. 32, B11; **Estimated GPS:** 41°36.77'N; 73°10.32'W
Views: Lateral of main falls; closer views of lower cascades halfway down from top of ravine

Aesthetics: Excellent
Characteristics: Remote, scenic, medium-sized
Accessibility: 0.4-mile hike
Degree of Difficulty: Moderately easy
Information: Trail map available at www.nonnewaugfalls.blogspot.com/2010/07/working-trail-maps-of-nonnewaug-falls.html

DESCRIPTION: Nonnewaug Falls, aka Leever Falls, is on the Nonnewaug River—a medium-sized stream which rises in the hills east of Bethlehem, eventually flowing into the Pomperaug River in Woodbury. Three separate cascades are encountered in a 0.05-mile-long section where the river drops over 100 feet. The main falls is 20 feet high, cascading dramatically into the mouth of the gorge. Two smaller cascades, close to one another, are located several hundred feet downstream where the ravine narrows appreciably. The upper of the two lower falls is a 4-foot-high cascade, followed by a 6-foot-high cascade.

HISTORY: In 2002 Dr. Harold Leever willed 50 acres of land at the falls to the Town of Woodbury and 12 acres of land near the falls to the Bethlehem Land Trust to ensure the waterfall's preservation for perpetuity.

The falls are named after Chief Nonnewaug, a Native American sachem. *Nonnewaug* is Mohican for "dry land."

On the opposite bank near the top of the falls is a bronze tablet erected in 1916 by members of the Nonnewaug tribe of Seymour to memorialize the chief. It reads TO THE MEMORY OF NONNEWAUG. LAST CHIEF OF HIS TRIBE. FRIEND OF HIS WHITE NEIGHBORS. WHO SLEEPS WITH HIS FATHERS NEAR THE FALLS WHO BEAR HIS NAME. Legend states that Chief Nonnewaug was buried at the site, although exactly where is not known.

DIRECTIONS: From Bethlehem (junction of CT 61 and CT 132) drive southeast on CT 61 (Bethlehem Road) for 3.3 miles. Turn sharply left onto Nonnewaug Road.

From west of Watertown (junction of US 6 and CT 61), drive north on

Nonnewaug Falls overflows with Native American lore.

CT 61 (Bethlehem Road) for 0.7 mile and turn right onto Nonnewaug Road.

Proceed north on Nonnewaug Road for 0.6 mile. Then turn right onto Hickery Lane and head east. After 0.1 mile, as the main road veers left, continue straight ahead onto a dirt road which passes by a private home on your left. Go roughly 200 feet until you reach the end of the road, which is barricaded. Park off to the side of the road, being sure not to block the road.

Proceeding on foot, walk past the barricade and follow the dirt road east. Take note of the signs on your right which read No TRESPASSING. PUBLIC WATER SUPPLY. You are fine as long as you stay on the road. In less than 0.1 mile bear right where the road forks, and continue uphill. After less than 0.1 mile you will pass by a kiosk on your left which contains information about the preserve.

Within 0.2 mile you will come to a *T* at the top of the hill. Go right for 0.05 mile until you come to another junction, where two enormous oak trees tower above the road. From here proceed straight ahead, cross an open field, and head toward a forest line of conifers. You will arrive at the top of the falls right after you enter the woods.

From the main falls follow a path downstream along the top of the gorge for several hundred feet, and turn left onto a side path that leads quickly down to an overlook above the two lower cascades, roughly halfway into the gorge. Do not try to descend farther.

31

MAD RIVER CASCADES

Location: Wolcott (New Haven County), Peterson Memorial Park

Delorme Connecticut/Rhode Island Atlas and Gazetteer: p. 33, C22; **Estimated GPS:** 41°36.65'N; 72°59.22'W

Views: Head-on, lateral

Aesthetics: Good

Characteristics: Remote, scenic, small, very picturesque

Accessibility: 0.3-mile walk

Degree of Difficulty: Moderately easy

Information: Peterson Memorial Park, 203-879-8100; trail map available in Ann T. Colson (ed.), *Connecticut Walk Book: The Guide to the Blue-Blazed Hiking Trails of Western Connecticut* (19th ed.), (Connecticut Forest & Park Association, 2006), page 134.

DESCRIPTION: A series of small cascades, 3–4 feet high, have formed on the Mad River—a medium-sized stream which rises from Cedar Swamp Pond and flows into the Naugatuck River at Waterbury. The cascades begin upstream at the mouth of a shallow, 25-foot-long flume, and continue around a bend in the river to where Break Hill Brook enters from the northwest.

Small cascades on the Mad River near its confluence with Break Hill Brook

HISTORY: The Peterson Memorial Park, created in 1963, contains 65 acres of land. The 35-mile-long Mattatuck Trail starts from the park and ends up at Mohawk Mountain State Park in Cornwall, joining with the Appalachian National Scenic Trail.

DIRECTIONS: From Wolcott (junction of CT 69 and CT 322) drive north on CT 69 for over 0.1 mile. When you come to Mad River Road turn left, and head northwest for 0.2 mile. Then turn right into Peterson Memorial Park and go 0.1 mile to the parking area left of the skateboard area. The Mattatuck Trail begins here.

Follow the Mattatuck Trail north for 0.3 mile to reach the cascades. A succession of footbridges take you across the river, and then back to the same side again.

32

HANCOCK BROOK CASCADES

Location: Waterville (New Haven County), Mattatuck State Forest **Delorme Connecticut/Rhode Island Atlas and Gazetteer:** p. 33, D19; **Estimated GPS:** 41°35.80'N; 73°02.87'W **Views:** Tributary to Hancock Brook—Head-on; Hancock Brook—Lateral from a distance **Aesthetics:** Good **Characteristics:** Remote, scenic, medium-sized

Accessibility: 0.2-mile walk to cascade on tributary; 0.1- to 0.4-mile hike along Hancock Brook past multiple tiny cascades **Degree of Difficulty:** Moderate **Information:** Trail map available in Ann T. Colson (ed.), *Connecticut Walk Book: The Guide to the Blue-Blazed Hiking Trails of Western Connecticut* (19th ed.), (Connecticut Forest & Park Association, 2006), page 334.

DESCRIPTION: A series of tiny cascades and rapids have formed on a 0.4-mile-long section of Hancock Brook, a medium-sized stream which rises from a pond east of Fall Mountain and flows into the Naugatuck River south of Waterville. Although none of the cascades are distinctive enough to be described individually, nor are any close enough to the trail to be readily accessible, the experience of hiking through this gorge is not one to be missed.

As it turns out, the main cascade is not on Hancock Brook, but rather on a tiny, unnamed tributary to Hancock Brook that rises from the east hills, producing a narrow 20- to 30-foot-high cascade as it drops into the gorge. What makes the hike following Hancock Brook upstream so exciting is the dramatic gorge that has been deeply carved out by a fast-moving, chattering stream. Its towering cliff walls loom high above the trail and stream. The Connecticut Forest & Park Association created the 2.8-mile-long trail system.

HISTORY: The brook is named after Thomas Hancock (possibly spelled Hancox earlier), an early settler.

Were it possible to continue following Hancock Brook northeast, you would eventually reach Buttermilk Falls near Tolles after roughly 4.5 miles (see entry on Buttermilk Falls [Tolles]).

DIRECTIONS: Heading south on CT 8, get off at exit 36 for Huntington Avenue and Colonial Avenue. At end of the ramp, turn left onto Colonial Avenue and drive less than 0.1 mile. When you come to Huntington Avenue turn left, proceeding under the CT 8 overpass.

Heading north on CT 8, get off at exit 36 and turn right onto Huntington Avenue.

Approaching from either direction, continue east on Huntington Avenue for 0.2 mile into Waterville. Then turn left onto Thomaston Avenue and head north for 0.3 mile. When you come to Sheffield Street, turn right and continue northeast until you reach a bluestone quarry at the end of the road at 0.5 mile.

Take note of the derelict, 56-foot-long, lenticular pony truss iron bridge spanning Hancock Brook near the parking area. The bridge, built in 1884 by the Berlin Iron Company, has been closed off for many years and is now on the National Register of Historic Places.

Proceeding on foot, follow the blue-blazed trail north along the west bank of Hancock Brook. For the first 0.1 mile the walk takes you across the spacious floor of the quarry. Upon reaching the edge of the woods, the trail's continuation is clearly evident.

Entering the woods, you will come to a secondary road at 0.05 mile. Follow it downhill for 200 feet to the stream below. The main cascade is on a tributary to Hancock Brook on the opposite bank, just downstream from where the secondary road has taken you.

Return to the main road/path and continue following the trail north as it heads deeper into the gorge. The road stays high above the stream for the first 0.3 mile; then moves down closer. High above you are impressive cliffs that frame the gorge. Look across the river to the top of the opposite bank, and you will periodically see a railroad line that was built between 1906 and 1907, connecting Waterbury to Hartford.

By the time you reach the 0.4-mile point, the trail and gorge are strewn with enormous boulders. After 0.5 mile the stream turns placid, which makes this a good point to turn around.

During your hike through Hancock Brook Gorge you will see numerous tiny cascades and rapids, but none are larger than 2–3 feet in height. The main cascade, it turns out, is the tributary coming into Hancock Brook.

33

See page 212 for hiking map

SPRUCE BROOK FALLS

Location: Beacon Falls (New Haven County), Naugatuck State Forest
Delorme Connecticut/Rhode Island Atlas and Gazetteer: p. 33, L17–18; **Estimated GPS:** 41°27.35'N; 73°03.78'W

Views: Head-on, lateral
Aesthetics: Excellent
Characteristics: Remote, scenic, medium-sized
Accessibility: 0.5-mile hike
Degree of Difficulty: Moderately difficult

DESCRIPTION: Spruce Brook Falls consists of at least seven distinct waterfalls and innumerable tiny cascades within a 0.3-mile-long section of Spruce Brook, a small stream which rises from the hills northwest of Beacon Falls and flows into the Naugatuck River. One of Connecticut's most beautiful natural areas is the stupendous gorge containing Spruce Brook.

HISTORY: Spruce Brook Falls is in the Naugatuck State Forest/West Block on 2,000 acres of land donated by the Whittimore family in 1931 to honor Harris Whittimore, an industrialist and member of the State Forest and Park Commission. Native Americans originally used the land for hunting. Years later, 18th century industrialists logged the land.

In 1876 the Naugatuck Railroad Company established High Rock Grove at the terminus of the brook; its line ran along the west bank of the Naugatuck River. The company built a railroad station where passengers could get off and enjoy the picnic grounds, croquet field, carousel, and skating rink, as well as go boating on the Naugatuck River. This was done both to promote business for the railroad and to accustom people to traveling by

One of the falls on Spruce Brook formed in a wild and dynamic gorge.

rail. High Rock Grove was named for High Rock—a mountainous area overlooking the village of Beacon Falls.

Hikers should be warned that a multiheaded serpent is said to wander the glen at midnight on two specific nights a year—March 20 and November 20. What's more, the serpent's origin is connected to the huge glacial boulder adjacent to the parking area. According to legend, a Native American chief named Toby had a daughter who refused to be traded for a jug of rum by her thoughtless father, and subsequently jumped off from a precipice near High Rock and killed herself. Her father, feeling terrible guilt and remorse, pitched his jug of rum off from the edge of the ledge. When the jug shattered below, the huge boulder by the parking area emerged from the earth—a monument to the girl, and a reminder of the evils of rum. The spirit of the dead girl now reappears twice a year in the form of a seven-headed serpent. So beware!

DIRECTIONS: From Waterbury heading south on CT 8, get off at exit 24 for Beacon Falls. Turn right onto North Main Street and proceed south for 0.1 mile until you reach Depot Street, on your right.

From Seymour heading north on CT 8 get off at exit 23 for Pine Bridge. Turn right onto South Main Street and drive north for 1.0 mile until you reach Depot Street, on your left.

Approaching from either direction, turn west onto Depot Street, crossing over an iron bridge. At the end of the bridge, turn right onto Lopus Road and drive north for 0.05 mile, coming immediately up to Cold Spring Road. Bear right onto Cold Spring Road and continue north for over 0.3 mile, reaching what initially appears to be the end of the road. From here, proceed north on a dirt road continuation of Cold Spring Road (which some maps list as High Rock Road) for 0.7 mile as it parallels the railroad tracks. When you come to a fork, bear left to reach a large parking area in another 0.05 mile.

Take note of an imposing boulder along the west border of the parking area (see history section for details). It is one of the largest boulders you will see in Connecticut. Looming high above, off in the distance, are lofty cliffs and bluffs. (Note: If you bear right at the fork instead, you will cross over Spruce Brook Creek and enter a larger parking area with kiosks—but then you will miss seeing the enormous glacial erratic.)

Proceeding on foot, follow a trail that leads from the north end of the parking area to Spruce Brook Gorge in 0.05 mile. Turn left and follow the trail upstream as it parallels the south bank of Spruce Brook. Within 0.05 mile you will begin seeing cascades which you will continue to encounter

Falls abound on Spruce Brook.

for another 0.2–0.3 mile. Depending upon how you count them, there will be at least seven falls.

Eventually you will reach a point where the stream flattens out. Continue following the trail uphill as it leads momentarily away from the gorge, which has now turned left around a bend. Within another 0.2 mile the trail comes back down to the stream. After another 0.1 mile of hiking look to your right across Spruce Brook and you will see a cascade formed on a tributary upstream from a small bridge.

Follow a side path that leads quickly down to Spruce Brook and rock hop across to the west bank of the stream. Walk over to the bridge which is part of a dirt road that parallels the west side of Spruce Brook.

From the bridge you can view several cascades that have formed in an impressively deep canyon. While a path on the left side of the canyon climbs steeply up to the top of the rim, there is little to be gained by making the effort to ascend, for the best views are those that have already been seen from the bridge at the bottom.

Back at Spruce Brook, were you to follow the dirt road upstream for another 0.2 mile you would pass by a small stone dam on the stream, but the road soon pulls away, and no further cascades are to be seen.

34

HOPP BROOK FALLS

Location: Bethany (New Haven County), Hopp Brook Tract
Delorme Connecticut/Rhode Island Atlas and Gazetteer: p. 24, B8; **Estimated GPS:** 41°25.99'N; 73°00.67'W
Views: Head-on

Aesthetics: Fair/Good
Characteristics: Remote, scenic, medium-sized, seasonal
Accessibility: 0.1-mile walk
Degree of Difficulty: Moderately easy

DESCRIPTION: This 15-foot-high, moss-covered cascade is on Hopp Brook—a small stream which rises from a small wetland area north of Bethany near the intersection of Lebanon Road and Fairwood Road and flows into the Bladens River east of Seymour. The cascade tends to be seasonal due to Hopp Brook's limited watershed of 3.3 square miles.

HISTORY: Bethany's Hopp Brook Tract consists of nearly 17 acres of land. Bethany is named after the biblical village of Bethany, Hebrew for "house of dates."

It's only a short hop to Hopp Brook Falls

DIRECTIONS: From Beacon Falls (junction of CT 42 and North Main Street), drive east on CT 42 (Bethany Road) for 1.1 miles. At the point where CT 42 swerves to the left continue straight onto Blackberry Road (later becoming Falls Road), heading east for another 1.6 miles. When you come to Pole Hill Road, pull over and park to your right.

From the southwest corner of Falls Road's intersection with Pole Hill Road, follow a trail which leads into the woods. In less than 0.05 mile you will pass by the cellar foundation of the A. T. Hotchkiss homestead to your right. In 0.1 mile further you will come to Hopp Brook where the cascade-bearing stream comes down to your right.

35

NAUGATUCK FALLS

Location: Seymour (New Haven County)
Delorme Connecticut/Rhode Island Atlas and Gazetteer: p. 24, D5; **Estimated GPS:** 41°23.60'N; 73°04.54'W
Views: Lateral
Aesthetics: Good

Characteristics: Urban, historic, medium-sized, broad, partially dammed
Accessibility: 25-foot walk to overviews from under the CT 8 bridge
Degree of Difficulty: Easy

DESCRIPTION: Naugatuck Falls is on the Naugatuck River, the largest river in the state that both begins and terminates within state boundaries. It rises south of Norfolk, and flows into the Housatonic River at Derby.

Naugatuck Falls is 15–20 feet high and impressively broad. Roughly 2/3 of it is natural; the other 1/3 is dammed. In 1850 French and Dwight replaced a timber and plank dam with one of solid masonry. The waterfall has also been known as The Falls, Little Niagara, Rimmon Falls, and Tingue Dam Falls.

HISTORY: By the mid-1600s, Native Americans had established a village named Nawcatock by the falls. In 1783 the village became known as Chusetown after Chief Joseph Mauwehu, a French and Indian War scout who was nicknamed Chuse.

In 1803 the name of the village changed again, this time to Rimmon

Naugatuck Falls has powered numerous mills over the centuries.

Falls, but only until 1805 when it was renamed Humphreysville in honor of General David Humphrey who fought in the Revolutionary War and who later ministered to Spain and Portugal. Humphrey learned about the fine wool of Merino sheep and decided to profit from this knowledge, building a large woolen mill near the falls in 1806. In 1850 the village changed its name for the final time to Seymour after Governor Thomas H. Seymour.

The river's name, *Naugatuck,* is Quinnipiac for "one large tree." That the river should be named for a tree holds a certain degree of irony.

DIRECTIONS: Heading north on CT 8 from Derby, get off at exit 22. At the end of the ramp turn right onto Wakeley Street, avoiding the left-hand turn which takes you to CT 67, and proceed south for less than 0.1 mile.

Just before you reach Fall View Apartments, turn right and drive west into a parking area overlooking the river. Wheel Park, designated for skateboarders, will be to your right.

Going south on CT 8 from Beacon Falls get off at exit 22. Turn right onto CT 67 and head southwest for 0.1 mile. Then turn left onto Columbus Street/First Street, and proceed south for less than 0.1 mile. When you come to DeForest Street, turn right and head west. Continue straight ahead past Fall View Apartments (to your left) and proceed directly to a parking area next to the river.

Walk over to the underbody of the CT 8 bridge from where great lateral views of the falls can be obtained. You are standing next to the former site of the Tingue Manufacturing Company.

To alternate viewing area: From the Fall View Apartments proceed east on DeForest Street for 0.1 mile. Turn right onto Main Street and head south for nearly 0.2 mile. Then turn right onto CT 313, crossing over a bridge spanning the Naugatuck River. At the west end of the bridge turn right and park immediately next to a small village park with historical markers. There are views of the falls from here, somewhat obscured by trees.

36

SOUTHFORD FALLS

Location: Southwest of Southbury (New Haven County), Southford Falls State Park
Delorme Connecticut/Rhode Island Atlas and Gazetteer: p. 32, L12; **Estimated GPS:** 41°27.53'N; 73°09.90'W
Views: Head-on, lateral
Aesthetics: Good
Characteristics: Scenic, small, partially dammed

Accessibility: 0.3-mile walk around perimeter of ravine containing the cascades
Degree of Difficulty: Moderately easy
Information: Southford Falls State Park, 203-264-5169; trail map available at www.ct.gov/dep/cwp /view.asp?a=2716&q=325266

DESCRIPTION: Southford Falls encompasses a series of small cascades at the outlet to Mill Pond, a small body of water created for industrial purposes. The cascades are formed on Eightmile Brook, a medium-sized stream which rises southwest from Lake Quassapaug and flows into the Housatonic River east of Stevenson. None of the cascades are sizeable, but collectively they make a favorable impression. Historians believe that the gorge below the mill pond was intentionally deepened at one time in order to increase the stream's speed and power.

The dam forming Paper Mill Pond is roughly 10 feet in height and spans the top of the cascades. Remnants of a large mill foundation can be seen near the bottom of the falls, including a 1972 replica built by Ed Palmer of an 1804 Burr arch covered bridge. Look for an old millstone at the west

Pomperaug Falls, little known outside of Woodbury

end of the bridge. Further downstream the river flows through a deeper gorge where no cascades are found.

HISTORY: Southford Falls is in the 120-acre Southford Falls State Park. The falling waters of Eightmile Brook once drove a flour mill, fulling mill, sawmill, gristmill, paper mill, button mill, cutlery shop, axe handle factory, blacksmith shop, and butcher shop. There was even a hotel where tourists could stay.

The first parcels of land were acquired by the State of Connecticut in 1926. Then in 1932 the Whittemore Company donated the upper portion of paper millpond and Eightmile Brook to the State of Connecticut. By 1948 all land acquisitions had been completed.

Little if any traces of the former mills remain today except for the foundation ruins of the Diamond Match Company. In 1901 the Diamond Match Company took over the Southford paper mill that had operated since 1855, and began making paperboard for matchbooks and matchboxes. In 1923 a suspicious fire destroyed the building six months after it had closed.

In 1934 the Civilian Conservation Corps (CCC) helped reclaim the land, clearing the wreckage from the gutted factory that lay strewn about. The parking lot used today by the park both housed employees and was the former site of the baseball field.

Southford's name is a portmanteau of Southbury and Oxford, two nearby towns.

Southford Falls, heavily industrialized in years past

DIRECTIONS: Driving along I-84, get off at exit 15 for Southbury and proceed southeast on CT 67 for nearly 3.0 miles to Southford.

Just past Southford, turn right on CT 188 and proceed southwest for 0.4 mile. Then turn left into the large parking area for Southford Falls State Park. A kiosk near the parking area provides considerable information about the site's history.

From the parking area, follow a gravel walkway south along the side of the millpond. Since trails follow along both side of the brook, from here you can do a loop—crossing over the millpond's outlet, walking down along the east bank to the covered bridge, and back up along the west bank.

ADDITIONAL CASCADE: Pomperaug Falls is a dammed, 10-foot-high waterfall at the mouth of a small but striking gorge on the Pomperaug River. *Pomperaug* is Native American for "place of offering."

Driving along I-84, get off at exit 15 for Southbury, and head north on US 6 toward Woodbury for roughly 3.4 miles. Turn left onto South Pomperaug Avenue, proceed northwest for over 0.3 mile, and then left onto Pomperaug Avenue. In 0.1 mile you will cross over a small bridge spanning the Pomperaug River; the waterfall is to your left (41°31.60'N; 73°12.63'W). Park as best as you can beyond the bridge and walk back for views.

37

KETTLETOWN BROOK CASCADES

Location: East of Lakeside (New Haven County), Kettletown State Park

Delorme Connecticut/Rhode Island Atlas and Gazetteer: p. 23, B21; **Estimated GPS:** 41°25.48'N; 73°12.44'W

Views: Lateral

Aesthetics: Fair

Characteristics: Remote, small

Accessibility: 0.2-mile walk

Degree of Difficulty: Moderately easy

Information: Kettletown State Park, 203-264-5678; trail map available at www.ct.gov/dep /cwp/view.asp?a=2716&q=325230

Fee: Modest parking fee from Memorial Day to Labor Day

DESCRIPTION: Kettletown Brook Falls consist of a series of tiny cascades formed on Kettletown Brook, a small stream which rises south of Southbury and flows into Lake Zoar. None of the falls are higher than 3 or 4 feet, the most impressive cascade being the one first encountered.

HISTORY: Kettletown Brook Falls is in the 605-acre Kettletown State Park, historically noted for its abandoned millrace, former garnet mine, and charcoal hearth sites, all dating back to the late 1700s to early 1900s when the area was a source of fuel for local foundries. The park's initial 455 acres were purchased in 1950 through funds left by Edward Carrington of New Haven.

The Pootatucks originally inhabited the land. They were an Algonquin tribe whose early traces disappeared underwater in 1919 when Lake Zoar (a dammed section of the Housatonic River) was created.

The name Kettletown came about after early settlers obtained the land from the Pootatucks by trading a brass kettle for it.

DIRECTIONS: Going southwest on I-84, get off at exit 15 for Southbury. At the end of the ramp turn left onto CT 67, and proceed southeast for less than 0.2 mile to Kettletown Road (CT 487), on your right.

Going northeast on I-84, get off at exit 15 for Southbury and follow the exit ramp, bearing right, to Kettletown Road (CT 487).

Approaching from either direction, proceed south on Kettletown Road (later becoming Maple Tree Hill Road) for 3.4 miles. When you come to Georges Hill Road, turn right and drive west for over 0.6 mile until you reach Kettletown State Park on your left. Follow signs that lead to the beach in 0.5 mile, where limited parking is available.

Pick up the trail at the left north end of the beach where Kettletown Brook flows into the lake. After 0.1 mile cross over Kettletown Brook via a footbridge and then begin following the blue/yellow-blazed Brook Trail as it parallels the east bank of Kettletown Brook. You will immediately see tiny cascades as you head upstream. There are no further cascades once you have gone 0.2 mile.

38

CEDAR MILL BROOK FALLS

Location: North of Stevenson (New Haven County), Jackson Cove Town Park
Delorme Connecticut/Rhode Island Atlas and Gazetteer: p. 23, C23; **Estimated GPS:** 41°24.69'N; 73°11.33'W
Views: Head-on
Aesthetics: Fair
Characteristics: Remote, small, seasonal
Accessibility: 0.05-mile hike

Degree of Difficulty: Moderate, trail ascends rather steeply
Information: Jackson Cove Town Park, 203-888-7413; trail map available in Ann T. Colson (ed.), *Connecticut Walk Book: The Guide to the Blue-Blazed Hiking Trails of Western Connecticut* (19th ed.), (Connecticut Forest & Park Association, 2006), page 72.

DESCRIPTION: Cedar Mill Brook Falls is an 8-foot-high, moss-covered block cascade on Cedar Mill Brook—a tiny stream which rises in the hills to the east and flows into Lake Zoar. This is a seasonal cascade with a limited watershed. Visit in the early spring or after heavy, prolonged rainfall.

HISTORY: The Stevenson Dam created Lake Zoar in 1919 when it impounded the Housatonic River so that Connecticut Light & Power could use it to generate hydroelectric power. The 10-mile-long lake is the fifth largest in the state.

DIRECTIONS: Going southwest on I-84, get off at exit 15 for Southbury. At the end of the ramp turn left onto CT 67 and proceed southeast for less than 0.2 mile to Kettletown Road (CT 487), on your right.

Going northeast on I-84, get off at exit 15 for Southbury and follow the exit ramp, bearing right, to Kettletown Road (CT 487).

Proceed south on Kettletown Road, then Maple Tree Hill Road, and then Jackson Cove Road for a total of 4.7 miles until you reach the Jackson Cove Town Park. If the park is open, drive to its southeast corner, following a dirt road that leads in several hundred feet to parking for hikers. There is no charge for parking here. The park facilities are for Oxford residents only, however; for this reason, proceed directly to the trailhead, bypassing the facilities.

Follow the blue-blazed Pomperaug Trail into the gorge. Then, before crossing the brook, follow a trail steeply uphill for 0.05 mile to the cascade.

39

See page 212 for hiking map

PRYDDEN BROOK FALLS

Location: North of Stevenson (Fairfield County), Lower Paugussett State Forest **Delorme Connecticut/Rhode Island Atlas and Gazetteer:** p. 23, B21; **Estimated GPS:** 41°24.16'N; 73°11.26'W

Views: Head-on, lateral
Aesthetics: Excellent
Characteristics: Remote, scenic, large
Accessibility: 1.5-mile hike
Degree of Difficulty: Moderately difficult

DESCRIPTION: Prydden Brook Falls is a substantial waterfall on Prydden Brook, a small stream which rises in the Paugussett State Forest and flows into Lake Zoar.

The main fall tumbles over a block of rock, dropping 20 feet. A number of smaller cascades continue down almost to the shoreline of Lake Zoar, a 975-acre reservoir created when the Housatonic River was dammed up near Stevenson in 1919.

HISTORY: The Connecticut Department of Energy and Environmental Protection manages Prydden Brook Falls, located in the 1,200-acre lower section of the Paugussett State Forest.

Prydden is an old English name, originating from Priding in the Wheatenhurst rural district of Gloucestershire County in England.

DIRECTIONS: From I-84, get off at exit 11. When you come to Mile Hill Road, turn right and drive north for less than 0.2 mile. Then turn right onto CT 34 (Washington Road), and proceed southeast for nearly 5.0 miles until you reach Great Quarter Road on your left, 0.1 mile before the junction of CT 34 and CT 111 at Stevenson. Head north on Great Quarter Road for 1.3 miles until you come to a cul-de-sac where you can park.

Proceeding on foot, follow the blue-blazed Zoar Trail to the right of the kiosk. The trail leads along the shore of Lake Zoar. In 0.6 mile you will be opposite Jackson Cove, a clearing visible across the reservoir (see entry on Cedar Mill Brook Falls). At 1.5 miles you will be near Prydden Brook Falls, where informal paths lead to the right and downhill to the falls. Take note, however, that the easiest way to reach Prydden Brook Falls is to stay on the main trail for another 0.05 mile and then, at a stream crossing, turn right onto a well-worn trail paralleling Prydden Brook that leads down to the falls

Prydden Brook Falls, a great hiking destination

in less than 0.1 mile (and from there, continuing all the way downstream to the shoreline of the lake).

Boaters frequently visit the falls, either mooring their watercraft in the tiny cove at the base of the cascades or along the small section of rocky land jutting out from the south side of the stream.

40

See page 213 for hiking map

FARMILL RIVER FALLS

Location: Shelton (Fairfield County), Far Mill River Park
Delorme Connecticut/Rhode Island Atlas and Gazetteer: p. 24, L3; **Estimated GPS:** 41°15.58'N; 73°05.85'W
Views: Head-on, lateral
Aesthetics: Good

Characteristics: Remote, historic, scenic, small
Accessibility: 0.3-mile hike
Degree of Difficulty: Moderate
Information: Trail map available at www.borntoexplore.org/trails /far_mill_river.htm

DESCRIPTION: These small, pretty cascades are formed on the Farmill River, a medium-sized stream which rises from a pond southeast of Monroe and flows into the Housatonic River south of Pine Rock Park. The cascades are contained in a scenic, rocky glen with much exposed bedrock. At the upper cascade the stream, once dammed for hydropower, drops several feet into a languid pool and then dashes over a second, smaller cascade into another pool. A number of old foundation ruins are evident along the way up to the cascades, and additional tiny cascades are located further upstream in different sections of the gorge.

HISTORY: Far Mill River Park consists of 46 acres of land. The gorge extends along a 1.9- mile length of river between River Road and Farmill Crossing.

The old ruins at the beginning of the hike are from the Roberts paper mill which burned down in 1907.

DIRECTIONS: Going south on CT 8 get off at exit 14 for Shelton, and turn left onto Howe Avenue (CT 110).

Going north, get off at exit 14 and turn left onto Kneen Street, and then immediately right onto Howe Avenue (CT 110).

The falls on Farmill River, just far enough upstream to seem secluded

Approaching from either direction, head south on Howe Avenue/River Road for 4.4 miles. Just before crossing over the Farmill River, turn right into the parking lot for ASF Sports and Outdoor (865 River Road) where trailhead parking is permitted.

Walk to the southwest end of the store's property and follow the Pine Rock Park Trail along the north bank of the river. You will quickly come upon old foundation ruins off to your left. In less than 0.3 mile you will reach a pretty glen with cascades, where a side path leads down to an area of exposed bedrock in 15 feet.

41

INDIAN WELL FALLS

Location: Northwest of Shelton (Fairfield County), Indian Well State Park
Delorme Connecticut/Rhode Island Atlas and Gazetteer: p. 24, G2; **Estimated GPS:** 41°20.33'N; 73°07.43'W
Views: Head-on
Aesthetics: Good

Characteristics: Historic, scenic, medium-sized
Accessibility: 0.1-mile walk
Degree of Difficulty: Moderately easy
Information: Indian Well State Park, 203-735-4311, 1-866-287-2757; trail map:www.ct.gov/dep/lib /dep/stateparks/maps/indianwell.pdf

DESCRIPTION: Indian Well Falls is a 12- to 15-foot-high waterfall on Indian Hole Brook, a small stream which rises west of Shelton and flows into the Housatonic River immediately east of the park. Adding to the waterfall's uniqueness is the large, open well (an enormous pothole) that momentarily captures the plunging stream before releasing it to continue downstream into the Housatonic River.

HISTORY: Indian Well Falls is in Indian Well State Park, named after the park's distinctive well-shaped pothole. It is reminiscent of the uppermost falls at Kent Falls State Park (see entry on Kent Falls).

In 1928 the state of Connecticut acquired 153 acres of land, including the waterfall, which was previously owned and run by Camp Irving, a Boy Scout camp.

The stretch of the Housatonic River parallel to the park was at one time a shipbuilding center. After the War of 1812 the center went into decline. When the dam at Shelton was erected, a substantial area of homes called "The Great Plains" ended up under Lake Housatonic.

As so often happens with large or distinctive waterfalls, the waterfall's history intertwines with a Native American tale. It is the familiar Romeo and Juliet story of an Indian princess who, in a fit of anguish over her forbidden love with a brave from a rival tribe, jumps off the top of the falls to her death. Considering the number of similar tales told, it's a wonder that enough Native American females survived to propagate the tribe's continuation.

DIRECTIONS: Driving south along CT 8 between Bridgeport and Seymour, get off at exit 14 for Shelton, and turn right onto Howe Avenue (CT 110).

Indian Well Falls, named for its awesome pothole

Heading north on CT 8, get off at exit 14, turn left onto Kneen Street, and then immediately left onto Howe Avenue (CT 110).

Approaching from either direction, proceed northwest on CT 110 (Howe Avenue) for 2.3 miles. When you see the sign for Indian Well State Park turn right and continue northwest on Indian Well Road for another 0.4 mile until you reach a large parking lot on your right.

From the parking lot, walk 50 feet north, cross the road, and follow a well-worn path along the south side of a small stream for over 0.1 mile. Where the stream does an abrupt right angle turn, you'll find the waterfall.

42

See page 213 for hiking map

WHITE HILLS BROOK CASCADES

Location: Northwest of Shelton (Fairfield County), Birchbank Mountain Open Space
Delorme Connecticut/Rhode Island Atlas and Gazetteer: p. 24, F1; **Estimated GPS:** 41°21.24'N; 73°08.47'W
Views: Head-on, lateral

Aesthetics: Good
Characteristics: Remote, scenic, small, seasonal
Accessibility: 0.5-mile hike
Degree of Difficulty: Moderate
Information: Trail map available at www.sheltonconservation.org /recreation/maps/Birchbank Map pdf

DESCRIPTION: Two pretty 10-foot-high cascades have formed on White Hills Brook—a small stream that rises in the White Hills above the Housatonic valley, and flows into the nearby Housatonic River.

The upper cascade is fairly elongated, dropping a total of 10 feet over a distance of 30 feet. The lower cascade is equally as high, but more steeply elevated.

HISTORY: The Birchbank Mountain Open Space consists of 155 acres of land encompassing a particularly scenic section along the Housatonic River. The land was purchased from the Bridgeport Hydraulic Company (now called Aquarion Water Company) in 1998.

The impressive bluff along the west bank of the Housatonic River, which rises some 300–400 feet above the valley floor, most assuredly would have presented a nearly impassable barrier to Native American and colonial travelers were it not for a convenient notch carved out by White Hills Brook.

This notch allowed farmers to haul down produce from the upper regions of the White Hills for export on the Housatonic River. The ascending white-blazed trail now follows this old route.

DIRECTIONS: Driving south along CT 8 between Bridgeport and Seymour, get off at exit 14 for Shelton, and turn right onto Howe Avenue (CT 110).

Heading north on CT 8, get off at exit 14, turn left onto Kneen Street, and then immediately left onto Howe Avenue (CT 110).

Approaching from either direction, proceed northwest on Howe Avenue for 2.3 miles. When you see the sign for Indian Well State Park, turn right and follow Indian Well Road (which later becomes Birchbank Road) northwest for 1.9 miles. Just before crossing a railroad track at the bottom of the hill where the floodplain starts, turn into a tiny parking area on your left that can accommodate two or three cars.

Head north on the white-blazed trail for 0.5 mile, following an old roadbed that once was Old Farm Road. At 0.4 mile the trail divides. Continue straight ahead for less than 0.1 mile farther. Before coming to where Upper White Hills Brook crosses the trail, follow an obvious path/old road to your left, which leads uphill to the cascades in less than 0.05 mile. The two cascades are separated by only 100 feet.

43

FALLS IN PEQUONNOCK RIVER VALLEY STATE PARK

Location: Trumbull (Fairfield County), Pequonnock River Valley State Park

Delorme Connecticut/Rhode Island Atlas and Gazetteer: p. 23, L21; **Estimated GPS:** 41°15.17'N; 73°12.06'W

Views: Head-on, lateral

Aesthetics: Good

Characteristics: Remote, historic, medium-sized

Accessibility: Cascade #1—0.7-mile hike; Cascade #2—1.0-mile hike

Degree of Difficulty: Moderately difficult

Information: Trail map available at www.trumbullhistory.org/valley/valmap.gif

DESCRIPTION: Several small cascades can be seen along the Pequonnock River, including one of its tiny tributaries. None of the cascades are particularly large, but you will be more than compensated by the awesome scenery of the gorge. The Pequonnock River rises northwest of Monroe, and flows into Bridgeport's harbor.

The initial part of the hike takes you past a number of tiny cascades in the river. The main attraction is a 20-foot-high cascade, on a tiny tributary to the Pequonnock River at a trail crossing. Further on is a small but distinctive cascade on the Pequonnock River, walled in by a small but impressive chasm.

HISTORY: The rapids and cascades on the Pequonnock River have been called "The Falls" since 1674. In the mid-18th century Gideon and Ephraim Hawley built a mill on the stream at a narrowing. Hawley's grandnephew, Daniel, later went on to erect a mill just north of Daniels Farm Road.

In 1826 three brothers, Reuben, Daniel, and Eben Fairchild, established the Fairchild paper mill at the falls of the Pequonnock River. It was the first mill to produce white notepaper. They were assisted by Andrew Tait, whose mill ruins are visible near the beginning of the hike.

From 1837 to 1840 William Peet and William C. Stirling constructed the Housatonic Railroad through the Pequonnock River Valley to link New Milford and Bridgeport. It consisted of the railroad line, two train stations, cow tunnels, bridges, and the Parlor Rock Amusement Park at the north end of the valley.

Sometime during the 19th century, Andrew Tait, who earlier helped build a paper and strawboard mill along the Pequonnock River, sold his property to the Bridgeport Hydraulic Company. They built a 135-by-75-foot ice house between the railroad and reservoir, 1.0 mile north of Trumbull Center.

In 1971 the U.S. Army Corps of Engineers conducted a feasibility study to evaluate the merit of constructing a 135-foot-high, 950-foot-long dam to create a reservoir that would back up the river for 2.5 miles. Fortunately for nature lovers it was never acted on.

In 1989 the town of Trumbull and the state Department of Energy and Environmental Protection purchased 382 acres of land in the Pequonnock River Valley from the Bridgeport Hydraulic Company to ensure its protection from further development.

Pequonnock is a Native American word, possibly meaning "cleared field," "broken ground," or "place of destruction."

DIRECTIONS: From CT 15 (the Merritt Parkway) in Trumbull, get off at exit 49 if you are driving west, or exit 49 north if you are driving east. Head north on CT 25 (the Colonel Henry Mucci Highway) for less than 1.0 mile and get off at exit 9. Turn left onto Daniels Farm Road, and proceed west for 0.05 mile. As soon as you cross over CT 25 turn right onto Park Street, and head north for 0.4 mile. You will come to a dead end where no parking is allowed; the trailhead starts here. Turn around and drive 0.1 mile back to a parking area on your right used by commuters. Then return to the trailhead on foot.

The blue-blazed trailhead begins from the kiosk at the end of Park Street. Within 0.05 mile you will cross over a tiny dam and then past the ruins of the 1836 Tait's mill. After a moment or two you will reach the Pequonnock River and begin following it upstream. Tiny cascades are evident along the river. As you continue the hike, you will be impressed by the immensity of the gorge, its sidewalls, and the large blocks of bedrock that are strewn about. In 0.6 mile you will reach the site of the old dam, spillway, and walkway bridge foundation. Look for a huge, rusted pipe—a relic from days when water poured through it. The height of the east wall of the gorge is particularly striking here. After another 0.1 mile the trail crosses over a stream in front of a gently sloping 20-foot-high cascade.

From this point on, the route ahead gets trickier. In addition to the blue-blazed trail you have been following, some of the intersecting trails are blazed yellow or white. In some places trail markers disappear entirely, victims of a maze of pathways that have been created by mountain bikers and ATVs.

At 1.0 mile you will come to the Black Pool and Falls area (GPS reading 41°15.85'N; 73°13.03'W), formed on the Pequonnock River. Centuries of turbulent waters sculpted and cut the bedrock deeply. Several semicircular potholes can be seen. A scenic gorge with pools of water contains the tiny cascade. Less than 0.05 mile downstream the stream cuts through a 15-foot-long, 25-foot-wide chasm. Looking upstream you will see that the opposite side of the stream has been reinforced by an extended wall of stone blocks.

FALLS ACCESSIBLE FROM CT 10

CT 10, combined with US 202, enters Connecticut from Southwick, Massachusetts. After passing through Tariffville, the two conjoined routes parallel the Farmington River, heading south. At Avon, a community named after the river that flows through Stratford-upon-Avon, England, US 202 veers off to the west leaving CT 10 to continue solo downstate.

Below Farmington, CT 10 follows along the Quinnipiac River and then

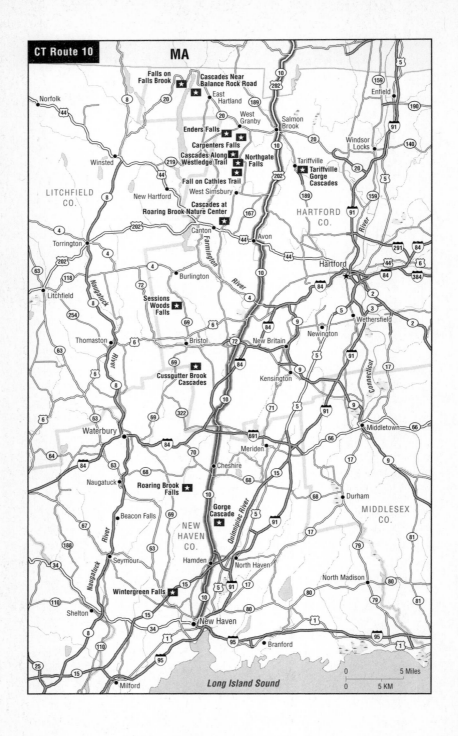

CT Route 10

MA

Falls on Falls Brook

Cascades Near Balance Rock Road

Norfolk

East Hartland

West Granby

Salmon Brook

Enfield

Enders Falls

Carpenters Falls

Cascades Along Westledge Trail

Northgate Falls

Tariffville

Winsted

Windsor Locks

Tariffville Gorge Cascades

LITCHFIELD CO.

Fall on Cathies Trail

New Hartford

West Simsbury

Cascades at Roaring Brook Nature Center

HARTFORD CO.

Canton

Avon

Torrington

Farmington River

Hartford

Burlington

River

Litchfield

Sessions Woods Falls

Naugatuck River

Thomaston

Bristol

New Britain

Wethersfield

Cussgutter Brook Cascades

Kensington

Newington

River

Waterbury

Middletown

Connecticut River

Naugatuck

Cheshire

Meriden

Roaring Brook Falls

Durham

MIDDLESEX CO.

Beacon Falls

Gorge Cascade

NEW HAVEN CO.

Quinnipiac River

Seymour

Hamden

North Haven

North Madison

Wintergreen Falls

Shelton

New Haven

Branford

Milford

Long Island Sound

5 Miles

5 KM

quickly switches over to parallel the Mill River. The roadway finally comes to an end when it reaches I-95 near New Haven harbor.

The main roads branching off east and west from CT 10 are CT 20 in Granby, US 44 in Avon, CT 72 in Plainville, and I-691 near Milldale. Some of these highways pass areas that are waterfall-bearing. By the time you reach New Haven, the east and west routes are simply too chaotic to be described here in one sentence by route numbers or by simple linear instructions.

44

See page 214 for hiking map

FALLS ON FALLS BROOK

Location: Northeast of West Hartland (Hartford County), Tunxis State Forest

Delorme Connecticut/Rhode Island Atlas and Gazetteer: p. 51, C24; **Estimated GPS:** 42°01.02'N; 73°57.15'W

Views: Lateral

Aesthetics: Good

Characteristics: Remote, scenic, medium-sized

Accessibility: 0.7-mile hike

Degree of Difficulty: Moderate

Information: Trail map available in Ann T. Colson (ed.), *Connecticut Walk Book: The Guide to the Blue-Blazed Hiking Trails of Western Connecticut* (19th ed.), (Connecticut Forest & Park Association, 2006), page 49.

DESCRIPTION: Two sizeable cascades are formed on Falls Brook—a small stream which rises near the Massachusetts/Connecticut border, and flows into the Barkhamsted Reservoir. The upper, accessible cascade is 20 feet high and surrounded by a rock garden of moss-covered boulders along its north bank and base. The lower waterfall is an elongated, 30-foot-high staircase of cascading water with a top visible from the upper cascade but inaccessible due to being on posted land.

These two falls are located in the western part of the Tunxis State Forest near the terminus of Falls Brook. A number of smaller cascades are encountered along the way down to the main falls. One source claims that the number totals 21—a figure that varies, no doubt, according to one's personal definition of a waterfall.

DIRECTIONS: From East Hartland (junction of CT 179 and CT 20), proceed northwest on CT 20. Along the way, at 4.5 miles, you will pass by an unnamed 30-foot-high seasonal cascade to your right. It is close to the roadside, but tucked away in the woods. At 5.4 miles you will come to a pullout on your left where a sign indicates the trailhead for the blue-blazed Falls Brook Trail.

Approaching from West Hartland (junction of CT 20 and CT 181), drive northeast on CT 20 for 3.4 miles. The trailhead and parking will be on your right, 1.0 mile after you pass by the sign for Granville State Park on your left.

From either direction follow the blue-blazed trail steadily downhill. In 0.3 mile you will come to the junction with the Falls Brook Loop Trail. Continue straight ahead, paralleling the north bank of the stream and passing by several small cascades as you head downstream.

In another 0.3 mile you will reach the southeast end of the loop trail, which crosses over the stream and returns on the opposite side. Continue straight ahead on what is now the white-blazed trail for 0.1 mile until you come to the top of the upper cascade.

The second cascade, whose top is visible just a short distance downstream, is on posted land, making it inaccessible.

Falls Brook's smorgasbord of waterfalls

45

CASCADES NEAR BALANCE ROCK ROAD

Location: West of East Hartland (Hartford County), Tunxis State Forest
Delorme Connecticut/Rhode Island Atlas and Gazetteer: p. 52, C2; **Estimated GPS:** 41°00.59'N; 72°55.29'W

Views: Lateral
Aesthetics: Fair/Good
Characteristics: Remote, scenic, small
Accessibility: 0.5-mile hike
Degree of Difficulty: Moderately easy

DESCRIPTION: A number of small falls have formed on a tiny creek which rises near May Pond and flows west into the Barkhamsted Reservoir. The falls consist of several cascades and slides, none greater than 3–5 feet in height.

HISTORY: These series of small cascades are surrounded by the 9,152-acre Tunxis State Forest, a large tract of unbroken woodlands occupying the towns of Hartland, Barkhamsted, and Granby. The Barkhamsted Reservoir overlays a 4.2-square-mile section of these lands.

Unlike parts of Vermont, whose forests were still growing back after being abandoned as farmland, much of the Tunix State Forest was already dense forest by the time the state acquired the lands in 1923.

DIRECTIONS: From East Hartland (junction of CT 20 and CT 179), go northwest on CT 20 (North Hollow Road) for 0.9 mile. Turn left onto Balance Rock Road and proceed west for 0.4 mile. Pull over along the side of the road just before reaching a cul-de-sac which is used as a bus turnaround today. No parking is allowed at the cul-de-sac.

Proceeding on foot, walk past the barrier at the end of the cul-de-sac and head west along the dirt road extension of Balance Rock Road for 0.2 mile. When you come to the blue-blazed Tunxis Trail marker, turn left and go southwest for 0.3 mile. Along the way you will cross over a tiny stream and then reach, within several hundred yards, a more substantial but still tiny stream. The path turns right here, paralleling the stream as the creek proceeds downhill for 0.05 mile, producing a series of small cascades to your left.

46

ENDERS FALLS

Location: West of West Granby (Litchfield County), Enders State Forest
Delorme Connecticut/Rhode Island Atlas and Gazetteer: p. 52, F5; **Estimated GPS:** 41°57.30'N; 72°52.74'W
Views: Head-on, lateral

Aesthetics: Excellent
Characteristics: Rural; scenic; small/medium-sized
Accessibility: 0.05- to 0.1-mile walk
Degree of Difficulty: Moderately easy

DESCRIPTION: Enders Falls consist of a series of cascades of varied shapes and sizes formed on Enders Brook—a small stream which rises in the swamps west of West Granby, and flows into the west branch of Salmon Brook.

The first waterfall is a 6-foot-high block cascade.

The second cascade has formed where the stream produces a 10-foot-high, three-tiered waterfall, the last two tiers of the cascade being formed where the stream exits through a 3-foot-wide narrowing in the bedrock. It is possible to scamper down to a quiet pool near the base of this waterfall for unobstructed views.

From here the stream drops over a near-vertical, 12-foot-high plunge falls into an area of still water. Steps lead down to close-up views of this section.

The next waterfall, 100 feet further downstream, is large and broad where the stream flows over a straightedge and then cascades down a 20- to 25-foot-high block nearly facing the trail.

The last falls, some 4 feet high, is 50 feet further downstream.

HISTORY: Enders Falls is in the Enders State Forest, established in 1970 through a land gift from the children of John Ostrom Enders and Harriet Whitmore Enders. Additional lands were acquired in 1981 and 2002, bringing the total up to 2,098 acres.

The falls are likely named after John Enders, whose hunting cabin (later owned by the Weeds, Lampsons, and Corrells) was moved from nearby Enders Road to its present location on Salmon Brook Street, 6 miles away. The cabin is now home to the Salmon Brook Historical Society.

DIRECTIONS: From Granby (junction of US 202/CT 10 and CT 20), go west on CT 20 (West Granby Road) for 3.7 miles, passing through Hug-

One of several cascades at Enders Falls

Enders Falls—a kaleidoscope of waterfalls

gins Gorge where the hills rise up nearly 500 feet above Salmon Brook. Turn left (west) onto CT 219 (Barkhamsted Road) and head southwest for 1.4 miles. Pull into the parking area designated for Enders State Park on your left.

Approaching from Barkhamsted (junction of CT 219 and CT 179), go northeast on CT 219 (Barkhamsted Road) for approximately 2.4 miles. Pull into the parking area for Enders State Forest on your right.

From the south end of the parking lot, walk past a barricade and follow an old road downhill for several hundred feet. The first falls is straight ahead where the road turns abruptly left and begins paralleling the west bank of the stream.

Follow the road and stream downhill for less than 0.1 mile as you go from one falls to the next.

47

CARPENTERS FALLS

Location: South of West Granby (Hartford County), Caruso-Collamore-Carpenter Preserve **Delorme Connecticut/Rhode Island Atlas and Gazetteer:** p. 52, G6; **Estimated GPS:** 41°56.79'N; 72°51.20'W

Views: Head-on
Aesthetics: Good
Characteristics: Remote, scenic, medium-sized
Accessibility: 0.05-mile bushwhack to view from base
Degree of Difficulty: Moderate

DESCRIPTION: Carpenters Falls, aka Carpenter's Falls, is a 15-foot-high cascade on Beach Brook—a small stream which rises on the west side of Weed Hill, south of West Granby, and flows into the west branch of Salmon Brook.

The top of the waterfall can be glimpsed by peering downstream from the east side of the Broad Hill Road bridge. Look closely and you will see a boulder in the streambed with a plaque announcing CARPENTERS FALLS.

Carpenters Falls, just a short distance downstream from the bridge

Immediately downstream from the base of the falls, Beach Brook turns sharply right, affording hikers who do a short bushwhack along the northeast bank an opportunity to come out to a head-on view of the waterfall.

HISTORY: Carpenters Falls is in the 382-acre Caruso-Collamore-Carpenter Preserve between Broad Hill and Weed Hill, part of the larger McLean Game Preserve in West Granby. The preserve is named after the Caruso, Collamore, and Carpenter families who, along with the Trustees of Frank Caruso at Bank of America, made this addition to the McLean Game Preserve possible through their generosity.

DIRECTIONS: From Granby (junction of CT 20 and CT 10/US 202), drive west on CT 20 (West Granby Road) for 2.8 miles. Turn left onto West Granby Street and proceed west for 0.1 mile. When you come to Simsbury Road bear left and drive south for over 0.05 mile. Then turn right onto Broad Hill Road, crossing over the west branch of Salmon Brook. Proceed south on Broad Hill Road, a seasonal road, for 0.9 mile until you come to a bridge. Park just before crossing over it.

It is also possible to drive in from the west end of Broad Hill Road. From the junction of CT 20 and CT 219 (west of West Granby), turn south onto CT 219 (Barkhamsted Road) and drive southwest for 0.5 mile. Turn left onto Broad Hill Road and proceed south for over 0.1 mile. Instead of bearing right onto Cone Mountain Road, proceed straight into the woods on Broad Hill Road, now a seasonal dirt road. In 0.9 mile you will come to an intersection. Turn right and park immediately next to the bridge spanning Beach Brook.

The waterfall is downstream from the bridge. The best way to reach the base of the falls is to follow the left bank of the creek downstream, a bushwhack of several hundred feet.

48

 See page 214 for hiking map

CASCADES ALONG WESTLEDGE TRAIL

Location: Midway between West Granby and West Simsbury (Hartford County), McLean Game Refuge
Delorme Connecticut/Rhode Island Atlas and Gazetteer: p. 52, 17; **Estimated GPS:** 41°55.06'N; 72°51.11'W
Views: Head-on, lateral
Aesthetics: Good
Accessibility: 0.2-mile hike

Characteristics: Remote, scenic, small
Degree of Difficulty: Moderate
Information: Trail map available in Ann T. Colson (ed.), *Connecticut Walk Book: The Guide to the Blue-Blazed Hiking Trails of Western Connecticut* (19th ed.), (Connecticut Forest & Park Association, 2006), page 156.

DESCRIPTION: A series of cascades have formed on a small, unnamed stream that flows into Bissell Brook. The uppermost waterfall is 8 feet high and drops steeply into a pretty pool. From here the stream rushes over two 4-foot-high slide cascades, and then a 3-foot falls where a narrow slot squeezes the stream to one side.

There are several tinier cascades as well as the main ones, all contained within a 200-foot length of streambed.

HISTORY: The upper part of the Westledge Trail follows along an 18th century stagecoach road past old stone walls and cellar holes, remnants of the once thriving village of Pilfershire. In early days the road provided an expedient way to get from Hartford to Albany.

The stone bench memorial to Deborah B. Eddy is near the trailhead. Eddy was an early environmentalist who served on the McLean Home and Game Refuge board for 21 years.

Bissell Brook, sometimes spelled Bissel's Brook, is named after John Bissell.

The Mclean Game Refuge, a collection of tracts of land, is named after George Payne McLean, an early 20th century U.S. senator and one-term governor of Connecticut. After leaving office McLean became active locally in wilderness preservation and began purchasing lands in the western hills of Granby using money he had inherited from an aunt. These purchases ultimately coalesced into the McLean Game Refuge, which now contains more than 4,800 acres of land.

Northgate Falls, virtually at the roadside

DIRECTIONS: From Granby (junction of CT 20 and CT 10/US 202), drive west on CT 20 (West Granby Road) for 2.5 miles. Turn left onto Day Street and drive south for 0.6 mile. When you reach Simsbury Road, turn left and proceed south for 0.6 mile. Then turn right onto Firetown Road and head south for nearly 2.0 miles. Just before you cross over Bissell Brook turn left into a small parking area for the McLean Game Refuge's Eddy Loop Trail.

Approaching from Simsbury (junction of US 202/CT 10 and CT 167), drive west on CT 167 (West Street) for 0.1 mile. Then turn right onto Firetown Road and head northwest for 4.6 miles. After crossing over Bissell Brook, turn quickly right into a small parking area for the McLean Game Refuge's Eddy Loop Trail.

From the parking area walk north along Firetown Road for less than 0.1 mile. Turn left into a private driveway (no parking is permitted here) and head west for about 100 feet. Then turn right onto the start of the pink-blazed Westledge Trail. Within 100 feet you will pass by the Deborah B. Eddy stone bench on your right. Continue following the trail (an old road) as it climbs uphill. In 0.1 mile you will come to a junction where the Westledge Trail continues straight ahead and the white-blazed Eddy Trail goes off to the right. Turn left here, following a faint, unmarked trail that leads

The Westledge Trail to a series of small cascades

over to the stream and uppermost cascade within several hundred feet. The downstream cascades require a short bushwhack, but once there all are within sight of one another.

ADDITIONAL CASCADE: Northgate Falls, aka Three Falls, is a medium-sized cascade on a tributary to Bissell Brook. The cascade contains three distinct drops totaling 30 feet, with a pool at the base of the bottommost cascade. Old foundation walls are visible along the east bank next to the lower falls. The ruins of an old stone dam can be seen above the uppermost cascade.

From the McLean Game Refuge's Eddy Loop Trail, walk straight across the road and follow a short path into the woods to reach Northgate Falls, clearly visible from the roadside. The trail ends at the top of a large stone wall overlooking the stream and cascades.

49

TARIFFVILLE GORGE CASCADES

Location: Tariffville (Hartford County), Tariffville Gorge
Delorme Connecticut/Rhode Island Atlas and Gazetteer: p. 52, 112; **Estimated GPS:** 41°53.90'N; 72°45.26'W
Views: Distant

Aesthetics: Fair/Good
Characteristics: Scenic, small, impressive gorge
Accessibility: 0.1-mile walk
Degree of Difficulty: Moderately easy

DESCRIPTION: "The Falls"—more dynamic rapids than cascades—are located on a section of the Farmington River earlier known as the Tunxis River. It was here where the power of moving water carved out an immense, 1.5-mile-long chasm called the Tariffville Gorge.

The 81-mile-long Farmington River, designated a natural and scenic river, rises from its west branch near Becket, Massachusetts, and east branch at the Barkhamsted Reservoir, and flows into the Connecticut River at Windsor. From the earliest times, the Farmington River proved to be so swift and deep that the river could only be safely forded at "The Falls" in Tariffville, and then only during low water.

The Tariffville Gorge—beloved by all who paddle its white waters

More recently the gorge has become a favorite playground for white-water paddlers, facilitated by a consistent flow of water throughout most of the year and coupled with the river's tendency not to freeze over in the winter. The section of Class III–IV white water in the gorge includes the famous "T-ville Hole." Pieces of the dam have acquired such colorful names as Car Rock and Aircraft Carrier.

HISTORY: The Farmington River presently flows into the Connecticut River at Windsor, but this wasn't always the case. Thousands of years ago the river continued south to Long Island Sound at New Haven, following a route that today has been usurped by the Quinnipiac River. When the last Ice Age ended some ten thousand years ago, huge glacial deposits at Plainville created a barrier that blocked the river's southward flow. An enormous lake formed, backing up 15 miles to inundate Avon, Farmington, and Simsbury. The waters, seeking a way to escape, finally broke through at a fault in the Talcott Mountain range and flowed east, now emptying into the Connecticut River. In the process, the stupendous gorge at Tariffville was cut.

Today the Farmington River comprises a watershed of 609 miles, with 14 major tributaries that feed into it, including the Still River, Roaring Brook, Hop Brook, Salmon Brook, Nod Brook, and Cherry Brook.

The falls were industrialized soon after settlers arrived in the area. In 1648 John Griffin established a factory for manufacturing turpentine, tar, pitch, and candlewood.

Tariffville was named after the Tariff Act of 1824.

DIRECTIONS: From Granby (junction of CT 189 and US 202/CT 10) drive southeast on CT 189 (Hartford Avenue) for 4.4 miles. Just before you reach a point where the highway divides and where a large, green, overhead sign indicates the way to EAST GRANBY/SUFFIELD 167N AND BLOOM-FIELD/HARTFORD CT 187 AND 189, turn left into an obvious pullout along the road.

From the parking area, follow a trail north upriver for 0.1 mile, bearing right where the trail splits. You will immediately come out to the Farmington River. Look upstream to see the breached dam, where a torrent of white water spills out near its north end. Across the river, just slightly downstream, are a series of rapids.

Hikers should take note that the blue-blazed Metacomet Trail follows along the ridgeline on the east side of the gorge, providing spectacular overlooks of the river and gorge.

50

 See page 215 for hiking map

WATERFALL ON CATHLES TRAIL

Location: Simsbury (Hartford County), Simsbury Land Trust
Delorme Connecticut/Rhode Island Atlas and Gazetteer: p. 52, I6; **Estimated GPS:** 41°53.97'N; 72°51.30'W
Views: Head-on
Aesthetics: Good

Characteristics: Remote, medium-sized, seasonal
Accessibility: 0.3-mile hike
Degree of Difficulty: Moderately easy
Information: Trail map: www.simsburylandtrust.org/pdf_files /slt_wlkbk_western_hilands_05.pdf

DESCRIPTION: This 30-foot-high waterfall is on a small stream which rises from West Mountain and flows into the headwaters of Bissell Brook. The cascade is fairly broad, with the narrow stream spreading out as it spills

The Cathles Trail leads to a striking seasonal cascade

over the top and drops down the rock face. At the base, the stream regroups and continues downhill.

HISTORY: The 47-acre Simsbury Land Trust's Cathles Property Trail wends its way between two nearby housing developments, and then climbs dramatically as it reaches the waterfall; from there it continues steeply uphill to the ridgeline at the southern end of West Mountain. The property lies between the McLean Game Refuge to the north and town open space to the east and south, and contains a "hidden valley" that runs north and south along a fault line.

Simsbury became an important mining area with the discovery of copper below Peak Mountain in 1705. This led to the development of the Simsbury Copper Mine, which later morphed into the notorious colonial penal colony Newgate Prison in East Granby.

Simsbury is named after the town of Symondsbury (pronounced *Simsbury*) in Dorset, England.

DIRECTIONS: From Simsbury (junction of US 202/CT 10 and CT 167), go west on CT 167 (West Street) for 0.7 mile. At the point where CT 167 turns left, continue straight ahead on CT 309 (Farms Village Road) and drive west for another 1.8 miles. When you come to Old Farms Road at a traffic light, turn right and proceed north for 1.7 miles. When you reach Lenora Drive, turn left and head west for 0.4 mile. Then turn right onto North Saddle Ridge Road and follow it north for 0.3 mile to a cul-de-sac.

Now proceeding on foot from the cul-de-sac, follow the white-blazed trail as it heads north through stone markers. In 0.3 mile the path leads up to the base of the cascade at the end of the town property.

51

CASCADES AT ROARING BROOK NATURE CENTER

Location: Northeast of Canton (Hartford County), Roaring Brook Nature Center

Delorme Connecticut/Rhode Island Atlas and Gazetteer: p. 43, A17; **Estimated GPS:** 41°50.34'N; 72°53.08'W

Views: Lateral

Aesthetics: Fair/Good

Characteristics: Historic, small

Accessibility: 0.5- to 0.8-mile hike (round-trip)

Degree of Difficulty: Moderately easy

Information: Roaring Brook Nature Center, 860-693-0263; trail map available at gift shop

Fee: None for walking the grounds; modest fee for touring the indoor nature center

Hours: Hiking trails open daily, dawn to dusk; nature center open Tuesday to Saturday, 10 AM to 5 PM; Sunday, 1 PM to 5 PM; closed Monday except during months of July and August

DESCRIPTION: Several small cascades are formed on Jim Brook—a tiny creek which rises west of Onion Mountain, and flows into a pond by Cherry Park. Don't expect to find a stream named Roaring Brook on the property, however—the name refers only to the nature center.

The blue-blazed Dish Mill Pond Trail leads past two artificial waterfalls. The first one is a dam at the south end of Werner Pond; the second is a breached stone dam that once impounded Dish Mill Pond.

The yellow-blazed Quarry Trail takes you past a series of small cascades and waterslides dropping 10 feet over a distance of 50 feet. The ravine is very rocky, with a proliferation of large boulders.

The Quarry Trail eventually leads past a stone quarry the Collins Company mined in the past. Some of the stone blocks quarried were used in the construction of the dam at Collinsville, where some quasi cascades can be seen.

HISTORY: Una Storrs Riddle founded the Roaring Brook Nature Center, originally called the Canton Children's Nature Museum, in 1948. In 1964 the name of the center changed to the Roaring Brook Nature Center. In that same year the State of Connecticut acquired 100 acres of adjacent lands encompassing the Werner farm. Through an informal agreement

Trails at the Roaring Brook Nature Center lead to cascades and dammed falls

with the Connecticut Department of Energy and Environmental Protection, the Werner farm property became available for the center to use for educational and recreational purposes. The present museum building was constructed in 1966. In 2002, the Department of Energy and Environmental Protection purchased 65 more acres of contiguous land, further increasing the land available for the nature center.

Jim Brook is named after James Baltimore, aka Jim Bell, who lived in Canton around 1774 and whose tenement was reputedly a resort for blacks.

The dam at the south end of Werner Pond replaces an earlier one built in the late 1800s. The old stone foundations of a dish mill can be seen near the breached stone dam at Dish Mill Pond. The mill scooped out wooden dishes using Jim Creek to power a lathe. Sections of this mill survived into the beginning of the twentieth century. As late as 1910 a waterwheel was still standing by the stream.

DIRECTIONS: From Avon (junction of US 202/CT 10 and US 44), drive west on US 44/US 202 (West Main Street) for 3.2 miles. When you come to CT 177 on your left, turn right onto Lawton Road and drive north for 0.9 mile. Then turn left onto Gracey Road, and proceed 0.4 mile north to the entrance to the Roaring Brook Nature Center.

Begin your hike from behind the nature center—not from the parking lot next to the building. Follow the red-blazed trail for over 0.1 mile as it leads you past Werner Pond and then crosses a walkway over a dam at the south end of the pond.

Once you reach the end of the walkway you have three trail options— the red-blazed Werner Pond Trail to the right; the yellow-blazed Quarry Trail to the left; and the blue-blazed Mill Pond Trail, which parallels the walkway, leading back toward the base of the dam.

Follow the blue-blazed trail to the cement dam (the artificial waterfall) and Jim Brook. From the Werner Pond dam, the trail takes you to a second artificial waterfall in less than 0.1 mile, which is the site of the old dish mill. After you have satisfied yourself looking at the ruins and dammed falls, return back to the junction of the three trails.

This time follow the yellow-blazed trail. In 0.05 mile the trail crosses a road (look out for passing cars) and then reenters the woods. Within a couple of hundred feet you will come to a fork. Go left, following the trail as it begins to parallel a lower part of Jim Brook. Within 0.1 mile after crossing the road you will come to several small, naturally formed cascades.

52

See page 215 for hiking map

SESSIONS WOODS FALLS

Location: South of Burlington (Hartford County), Sessions Woods Wildlife Management Area
Delorme Connecticut/Rhode Island Atlas and Gazetteer: p. 42, H12; **Estimated GPS:** 41°43.90'N; 72°57.35'W
Views: Head-on
Aesthetics: Fair/Good
Characteristics: Remote, scenic, small

Accessibility: 1.5-mile hike
Degree of Difficulty: Moderately difficult
Information: Sessions Woods Wildlife Management Area, 860-675-8130; trail map available at www.ct.gov/dep/lib/dep/wildlife/pdf_files/maps/maps_other/sw trail.pdf

DESCRIPTION: Sessions Woods Falls, aka Fall Brook Falls and Negro Hill Brook Falls, is on Falls Brook (formerly called Negro Hill Brook)—a medium-sized stream which rises west of Lamson Corner and flows into Copper Mine Brook northeast of Bristol.

The hike follows a gravel road with a number of ups and downs. A side path, ending with wood-lined earthen steps, leads down to the waterfall. The waterfall flows over blackened granite boulders, dropping 15 feet through a rock-choked gorge. Tiny cascades can be seen above the main falls as the stream makes its way through a field of boulders.

An old, 4-by-5-foot foundation wall set into the ground is approximately 50 feet from the brook, just slightly upstream from the top of the falls.

HISTORY: Sessions Woods Falls is in the Sessions Woods Wildlife Management Area, a 455-acre preserve established to demonstrate wildlife and resource management techniques. The State of Connecticut acquired the property from the United Methodist Church in 1981 through sportsmen-generated federal wildlife restoration funds.

DIRECTIONS: From Bristol (junction of US 6 and CT 69), head north on CT 69 (Burlington Avenue) for 3.7 miles. Turn left into the entrance at the Sessions Woods Wildlife Management Area and, after 0.1 mile, park in the main area to your left, directly in front of the Sessions Woods Conservation Education Center.

Sessions Woods Falls, just one of several attractions at the Sessions Woods Wildlife Management Area

To reach Sessions Woods Falls follow the Beaver Dam Trail (the main, 2.6-mile-long gravel road loop), for 1.3 miles. The Beaver Dam Trail can be accessed from either the right or left side of the education center. The side trail leading to the waterfall is found at approximately the halfway point along the Beaver Dam Trail, several hundred feet south of the Fire Tower Trail. It leads down to the base of the falls within 0.2 mile.

53

CUSSGUTTER BROOK CASCADES

Location: South of Bristol (Hartford County) **Delorme Connecticut/Rhode Island Atlas and Gazetteer:** p. 34, A2; **Estimated GPS:** 41°38.67'N; 72°55.42'W **Views:** Head-on, lateral **Aesthetics:** Fair **Characteristics:** Remote, scenic, small, poorly defined cascades

Accessibility: 0.4-mile hike **Degree of Difficulty:** Moderately difficult **Information:** Trail map available in Ann T. Colson (ed.), *Connecticut Walk Book: The Guide to the Blue-Blazed Hiking Trails of Western Connecticut* (19th ed.), (Connecticut Forest & Park Association, 2006), page 316.

DESCRIPTION: A number of small cascades and drops have formed on Cussgutter Brook—a small stream which rises near the border between the counties of Hartford and New Haven, and flows into Eightmile River north of Grannis Pond. The effect of cascading water becomes especially pronounced when you reach a section where water tumbles down 300 feet through a steeply inclined rock garden. This section has been given such colorful appellations as "The Chute" and "Purgatory."

DIRECTIONS: From southeast of Bristol (junction of CT 72 and CT 229) head southeast on CT 229 (Middle Street) for 0.1–0.3 mile, the mileage varying slightly depending on whether you took the Broad Street or Pine Street CT 72. (Both will get you to CT 229 at almost the same place).

Turn right onto Lake Avenue, and drive south for 1.5 miles. Just before you reach the service entrance to the Lake Compounce Family Theme Park (America's oldest amusement park) pull over to your right off the road by the trailhead, which is difficult to see unless you look closely. There is just enough room for three cars to pull off onto the grass above the curb.

Follow the blue-square/red-dot rail markers west for nearly 0.3 mile, paralleling the tiny stream which will be on your left. When you reach a junction with the blue-square/yellow-dot trail, coming in on your right, continue straight ahead on the blue-square/red-dot trail for another 0.05 mile. You will come to a section of the stream where the creek tumbles down through a rock garden of boulders. There are no distinctive cascades, but a general sense of falling water permeates the area.

From the base of the cascades, the blue-square/red-dot trail makes it way up through the boulder-choked gorge, providing lateral views of the cascading stream. At the top the trail continues to follow along the stream as it continues farther west.

54

See page 216 for hiking map

ROARING BROOK FALLS

Location: Southwest of Cheshire (New Haven), Roaring Brook Falls Natural Area
Delorme Connecticut/Rhode Island Atlas and Gazetteer: p. 34, K1; **Estimated GPS:** 41°28.89'N; 72°55.95'W
Views: Lateral, nearly head-on view from rim of gorge

Aesthetics: Excellent
Characteristics: Remote, scenic, robust, large, tall
Accessibility: 0.6-mile hike
Degree of Difficulty: Moderately difficult due to steep ascent
Information: Trail map available at kiosk

DESCRIPTION: Roaring Brook Falls is on Roaring Brook—a medium-sized stream which rises from hills east of Prospect and flows into the Mill River after joining with Willow Brook. The tallest single-drop falls in the state, the waterfall is 80 feet high. Additional cascades are visible both above and below the main falls, including a picturesque 10-foot-high cascade 0.05 mile upstream from the main falls.

HISTORY: Except for an old mill that once utilized Roaring Brook for waterpower, the lands have essentially been used strictly for farming.

In 1978 the town of Cheshire acquired the property encompassing Roar-

Roaring Brook Falls as it looked one hundred years ago (postcard)

ing Brook through the generous financial help of local residents, private clubs, civic groups, and the federal Heritage Conservation and Recreation services. Thomas P. Pool spearheaded much of this effort; a memorial plaque can be seen on the way up to the falls. In addition, Lawrence Copeland, who owned the property at that time, made a generous donation, as did the George W. Seymour Trust Fund.

Roaring Brook Falls, Connecticut's highest single-drop waterfall

There is no question that the size of Roaring Brook Falls can be intimidating. One can only imagine what it must feel like to be the size of an ant on a leaf about to go over the brink of the waterfall.

DIRECTIONS: *Land trust access:* From south of Cheshire at Richards Corner (junction of CT 10 and CT 42), drive west on CT 42 (Brooksvale Road) for 1.4 miles and turn right onto Mountain Road.

From north of Bethany (junction of CT 42 and CT 69), drive northeast on CT 42 for 2.6 miles and turn left onto Mountain Road.

Approaching from either direction, head north on Mountain Road for over 0.3 mile. Then turn left onto Roaring Brook Road and drive west for 0.1 mile to a cul-de-sac. Park in a small area to your right, next to the kiosk.

Proceeding on foot, follow a gravel road that leads past a pond and tennis courts. After walking less than 0.1 mile bear left, following the red-blazed markers. You will soon pass by a surviving 30-foot-high chimney whose fireplace is large enough to walk into. Immediately past the chimney the trail crosses over Roaring Brook, and then past a small monument on the left commemorating Thomas Pool, whose visionary work led to the acquisition and preservation of Roaring Brook Falls. From here, the trail proceeds steeply uphill, eventually reaching a crest, where it descends momentarily—only to start up again to a cleared area with a bench and spectacular views of the falls from atop the south bank. There is no reason to risk a descent into the gorge for a better view.

To see the upper cascades, continue climbing along the red-blazed trail. Along the way several small falls will be visible in the gorge to your right.

After cresting the top of the hill you will reach a junction where the blue-blazed Quinnipiac Trail comes in on your left. Continue straight ahead, following the stream for less than 0.05 mile to where it turns sharply right. You will immediately come to a pretty 10-foot-high cascade.

Quinnipiac Trail access: From south of Cheshire at Richards Corner (junction of CT 10 and CT 42) drive southwest on CT 42 for 2.9 miles. Park in a small area to your left, approximately 0.2 mile before Candee Road enters on the right. From here, follow the blue-blazed Quinnipiac markers that lead to the top of Roaring Brook Falls, a distance of over 1.0 mile. In order to properly see the waterfall, however, it will be necessary to descend 0.05 mile via the red-blazed trail to the main overlook. Hikers should be forewarned that it is a fairly steep descent.

55

GORGE CASCADE FALLS

Location: North of Hamden (New Haven County), Sleeping Giant State Park
Delorme Connecticut/Rhode Island Atlas and Gazetteer: p. 25, B16; **Estimated GPS:** 41°26.28'N; 72°53.55'W
Views: Lateral
Aesthetics: Fair

Characteristics: Remote, medium-sized, seasonal
Accessibility: 0.2-mile hike
Degree of Difficulty: Moderate
Information: Sleeping Giant State Park, 203-789-7498; trail map available at kiosk and at www.ct.gov/dep/lib/dep/stateparks /maps/sleepgiant.pdf

DESCRIPTION: The Gorge Cascade is a 25-foot-high cascading stream, with a distinct drop near its top, on a tiny tributary to a relatively insubstantial stream that flows along the bottom of the gorge and into the Mill River. This is a waterfall that only struts its stuff in the spring.

HISTORY: Gorge Cascade is in the Sleeping Giant State Park, a preserve established in 1924 by private patrons to ensure that the mountain would not succumb to traprock quarrying, an activity which had already started on the park's western corner. Fortunately all quarrying activities ceased in 1928, no doubt spurred on by the efforts of preservationists.

Since then the park has grown to encompass nearly 1,500 acres of land, including 32 miles of trails. Norman Greist and Richard Elliot, members of the Sleeping Giant Park Association, designed the elaborate looped-trail system.

The park's unusual name arose from the West Rock Range which, when viewed from the proper perspective, distinctly resembles a large recumbent man—hence the name Sleeping Giant.

DIRECTIONS: From Hamden (junction of CT 10 and the terminus of CT 40), drive north on CT 10 for 1.2 miles.

To pick up park map: Turn right onto Mt. Carmel Avenue, driving east for 0.2 mile, and then turn left into the main parking area for Sleeping Giant State Park. Maps can be obtained at the kiosk.

To reach the trailhead: From Mt. Carmel Avenue continue north on CT 10 for another 0.5 mile. Then turn right onto Tuttle Avenue and drive northeast for 1.0 mile. Park to your right in a small area large enough to accommodate four or five cars.

From the parking area, follow a trail paralleling a small creek for several hundred feet, and then bear right onto the red-blazed Gorge Trail. It ascends quickly and then parallels the rim of the gorge. In less than 0.2 mile you will come to a medium-sized, seasonal cascade that drops into the gorge. A tiny bridge crosses its top. If you look down into the gorge you will see, far below on the main stream, a small cascade and what appears to be a very elongated waterslide.

56

WINTERGREEN FALLS

Location: Northwest of New Haven (New Haven County), West Rock Nature Center

Delorme Connecticut/Rhode Island Atlas and Gazetteer: p. 24, G12; **Estimated GPS:** 41°20.80'N; 72°58.06'W

Views: From top

Aesthetics: Good

Characteristics: Remote, medium-sized

Accessibility: 200-foot walk

Degree of Difficulty: Easy

Information: West Rock Nature Center, 203-946-8016; trail maps available at http://www.ct.gov/dep/lib/dep/stateparks/maps/westrock.pdf

DESCRIPTION: Wintergreen Falls is a 25-foot-high cascade on Wintergreen Brook—a small stream which rises from Lake Wintergreen and flows into the West River southeast of Westville.

HISTORY: The falls is at the entrance to the 40-acre West Rock Nature Center, and formed at the head of a small gorge made out of hard traprock.

The nature center started in 1946 at the urging of Tony Cosenza after the New Haven Board of Park Commissioners asked him to run scout camping. For the next 31 years Cosenza and his wife, Virginia, worked arduously to make the natural area a viable outdoor learning center. The West Rock Nature Center was the first urban nature center in the country. In 2003 the Connecticut Historical Commission listed the West Rock Nature Center on the State Register of Historic Places.

DIRECTIONS: Traveling along CT 15 near New Haven, get off at exit 60. Head south on CT 10 (Dixwell Avenue) for roughly 1.6 miles. Turn right on Woodin Street, then immediately right again at a fork, still on

Wintergreen Falls, next to the West Rock Nature Center

Woodin Street, and head west for 1.7 miles. When you come to Wintergreen Avenue turn left and proceed south for 0.6 mile. As soon as you drive under the CT 15 overpass, turn left into a parking area at the entrance to the West Rock Nature Center.

Follow a footpath for 200 feet that leads downhill to the top of the falls. While it is possible to scramble down into the ravine for a head-on view of the waterfall, it is a tricky descent and best left to those who are sure-footed.

FALLS ACCESSIBLE FROM I-91

From Windsor Locks, I-91 follows along the west side of the Connecticut River, heading south through Hartford down to East Berlin (which is near the geographical center of Connecticut). At this point, I-91 pulls away dramatically from the Connecticut River, totally bypassing Middletown (a city which, back in the late 1700s, was the largest and wealthiest town in Connecticut) and skirting the east side of Meriden (a city dominated by traprock ranges to the east and west). From here, the interstate continues south and slightly west, now paralleling the Quinnipiac River, until it reaches the sandy plain of New Haven and I-95 next to New Haven harbor.

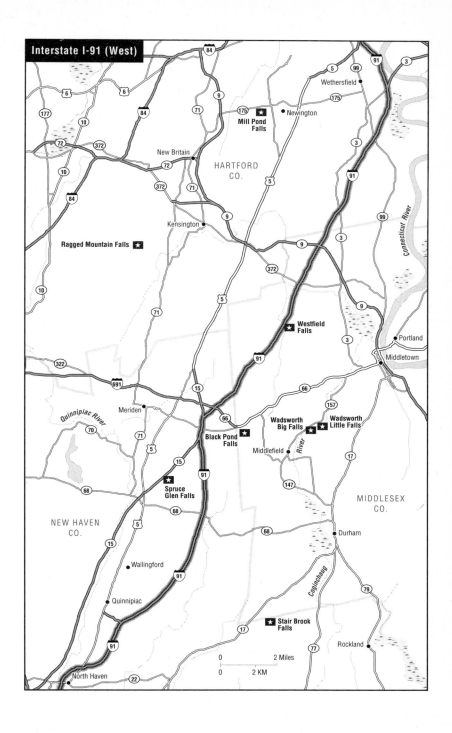

Interstate I-91 (West)

Wethersfield

Newington

Mill Pond Falls

New Britain

HARTFORD CO.

Kensington

Ragged Mountain Falls

Portland

Middletown

Westfield Falls

Meriden

Wadsworth Big Falls

Wadsworth Little Falls

Black Pond Falls

Middlefield

Spruce Glen Falls

MIDDLESEX CO.

Durham

NEW HAVEN CO.

Wallingford

Quinnipiac River

Quinnipiac

Coginchaug

Stair Brook Falls

Rockland

North Haven

Connecticut River

River

0   2 Miles
0   2 KM

57

MILL POND FALLS

Location: Newington (Hartford
County), Mill Pond Park
**Delorme Connecticut/Rhode
Island Atlas and Gazetteer:**
p. 44, J2; **Estimated GPS:**
41°41.63'N; 72°43.90'W
Views: Head-on

Aesthetics: Good
Characteristics: Urban, historic,
medium-sized
Accessibility: 100-foot walk
across level ground; wheelchair
accessible
Degree of Difficulty: Easy

DESCRIPTION: Mill Pond Falls is a 15-foot-high waterfall on Mill Brook—a small stream starting from Mill Pond and flowing into Piper Brook in a swampy area north of Newington. An iron-framed footbridge spans the top of the waterfall, giving it a pastoral look. Directly in front a railed viewing area, complete with benches, ensures that visitors can leisurely contemplate the falls. Mill Pond, directly above the falls, is encircled by a paved walkway.

HISTORY: Mill Pond Falls was named after a sawmill built on Mill Brook in 1860. In 2000 the Newington Waterfall Committee was formed to run an annual Waterfall Festival each September in the center of town.

DIRECTIONS: From southwest of Hartford (junction of I-84/US 6 and CT 9) drive south on CT 9 and get off at exit 29. Follow signs that direct you to CT 175 (Cedar Street) by going east on Ella T. Grasso Road for 100 feet, turning right onto Fenn Road, and then heading south for 0.05 mile.

Driving north on CT 9 between New Britain and the junction of CT 9 with I-84/US 6, get off at exit 29, which leads directly to CT 175 (Cedar Street).

Approaching from either direction, head east on CT 175 (Cedar Street) toward Newington Center for 1.2 miles. Then turn right onto CT 173 (Willard Avenue) and go south for less than 0.2 mile. When you come to Garfield Street, turn sharply left to enter Mill Pond Park. In less than 0.05 mile you will come to the parking area on your right. The waterfall is virtually next to the parking area.

Mill Pond Falls—a gem on the ringed walkway around Mill Pond

58

RAGGED MOUNTAIN CASCADE

Location: West of Kensington (Hartford County), Ragged Mountain Preserve
Delorme Connecticut/Rhode Island Atlas and Gazetteer: p. 34, A9; **Estimated GPS:** 41°37.70'N; 72°48.23'W
Views: Head-on, lateral
Aesthetics: Good

Characteristics: Remote, scenic, seasonal, amphitheater of traprock
Accessibility: 0.9-mile hike
Degree of Difficulty: Moderately difficult
Information: Trail map available at www.berlinlandtrust.org/activities .html

DESCRIPTION: This seasonal, 40-foot-high cascade is on an unnamed stream that runs down from the upper slopes of Ragged Mountain. The waterfall drops over a series of basalt ledges, the last drop being the most impressive of the ledges.

The cascade literally plummets into a huge amphitheater of loose traprock, the enormity of which has to be experienced to be appreciated. Two stone retaining walls, one above the other, are visible midway down the south side of the cascade. This area has all the appearance of having once been a quarry.

HISTORY: Ragged Mountain is part of the narrow, linear Metacomet Ridge that extends from Long Island Sound to the Vermont border. Basalt, a volcanic rock also known as traprock, makes up the 761-foot-high mountain. Because of its formidable rock walls, Ragged Mountain has been a mecca for rock climbers since the 1930s.

DIRECTIONS: From New Britain (junction of CT 372 and CT 71A) go south on CT 71A (Chamberlain Highway) for 1.1 miles.

From Meriden, going east on I-691, get off at exit 5 and head north on CT 71 (Chamberlain Highway) for 4.6 miles. Turn left onto CT 71A and continue north for another 1.2 miles. (If you are heading west on I-691, get off at exit 6, take Lewis Avenue north for over 0.2 mile, and then Kensington Avenue west for over 0.5 mile in order to get onto CT 71. Then drive north onto CT 71 for 4.2 miles, left onto CT 71A, and continue north for 1.2 miles.)

Approaching from either New Britain or Meriden, turn west onto West Lane and proceed west for 0.6 mile, pulling into the fairly extensive parking for the preserve on your right.

Head out on a trail (an old road) from the parking area for several hundred feet to reach the main loop trail. Turn right and follow the blue-blazed/red-dot trail north for nearly 0.9 mile. At 0.2 mile you will rock hop over a stream which can be easily forded under normal circumstances. From here the trail begins ascending. At 0.3 mile you will cross over a tiny stream contained in a gully that looks unnaturally straight, much like a canal.

After 0.8 mile you will come to the top of the Ragged Mountain cascade. The blue-blazed/red-dot trail descends steeply by the waterfall, eventually coming out in another 0.05 mile below the base of the cascade. Be prepared for a tricky descent, as the trail travels over loose traprock.

59

WESTFIELD FALLS

Location: West of Middletown (Middlesex County)

Delorme Connecticut/Rhode Island Atlas and Gazetteer: p. 35, E15; **Estimated GPS:** 41°34.80'N; 72°42.91'W

Views: From top—lateral; from base—head-on, lateral

Aesthetics: Good

Characteristics: Rural, medium-sized

Accessibility: Short walk across level ground to overlook of falls; 50-foot descent along short trail to lower section for more close-up views

Degree of Difficulty: Easy to moderately easy

DESCRIPTION: Westfield Falls is on Fall Brook—a medium-sized stream which rises from the Mt. Higby Reservoir and flows into Sawmill Brook just downstream from the falls. There are two distinct waterfalls adjacent to one another on the same stream, separated by a raised section of bedrock in the middle of the creek. The northmost fall is slightly taller than its companion, but neither waterfall is much higher than 20 feet. Depending upon water flow, a third waterfall will sometimes make an appearance. A small, flumelike cascade is visible immediately below the two falls.

Westfield Falls—two parallel falls on the same stream

DIRECTIONS: From I-91, going north, get off at exit 20 for Country Club Road and Middle Street, and turn right onto Country Club Road. Go southeast for several hundred feet.

From I-91, going south, get off at exit 20. Turn left onto Middle Street and then, within 0.1 mile, left onto Country Club Road. Go southeast for over 0.2 mile.

When you come to Miner Street, turn left and proceed northeast for nearly 0.9 mile. Miner Street parallels I-91 but at a slightly higher elevation. Pull into a tiny parking space on your left just before crossing over Fall Brook. Several large blocks of stone mark the pullout, undoubtedly placed there to limit the number of cars and visitors. A fairly deep gorge to your left is readily apparent.

Walk north along the top of the bedrock to reach an impressive overlook. To reach the bottom of Westfield Falls, follow a secondary path downhill from the stone blocks—a short walk of no more than a couple of hundred feet.

60

BLACK POND FALLS

Location: East of Meriden (on the border between Middlesex and New Haven Counties)
Delorme Connecticut/Rhode Island Atlas and Gazetteer: p. 35, H13; **Estimated GPS:** 41°31.63'N; 72°44.55'W
Views: From trail—Limited view near top of cascade; bushwhack to base—Head-on

Aesthetics: Poor/Fair
Characteristics: Remote, small, seasonal
Accessibility: 0.2-mile hike
Degree of Difficulty: Trail—easy to top, difficult descent to bottom; short bushwhack—moderate

DESCRIPTION: Black Pond Falls is a 15-foot-high seasonal cascade on a tiny tributary that drops down a talus slope into Black Pond. An accumulation of trash in the ravine, including a rusted automobile, has unfortunately marred the falls' pristine appearance!

Black Pond, covering 76 acres, is between the northwest end of the Beseck Mountain ridge and the south end of the Higby Mountain ridge at an elevation of 381 feet. Because of steep hills virtually surrounding it, the lake looks as though it formed in the cone of a volcano.

HISTORY: Although Black Pond Falls is on too insubstantial a creek to have an industrial history associated with it, a sawmill and gristmill were established in the 19th century on Black Pond Brook, roughly 0.5 mile northwest of Black Pond.

Nearby Meriden is a large town dominated by the Hanging Hills to the west and Mt. Lamentation to the east—both traprock ranges.

DIRECTIONS: From CT 15 at Meriden, get off at exit 67 and proceed east on East Main Street for roughly 1.2 miles. When you see a sign for a boat launch, turn right onto Black Pond Road and head downhill.

Two options present themselves for accessing the cascade.

Trail approach to top: Driving down Black Rock Road, pull off to your left at a barricaded, abandoned road at 0.15 mile. Now proceeding on foot, follow the abandoned road as it winds its way south around the east side of the lake, staying about 75 feet above Black Pond. In 0.2 mile you will come to a junction with the blue-blazed Mattabasset Trail. The cascade is off in the gully to your right here, with limited views from the top. If you wish to see the falls from the bottom the problem is getting down to the base. The slope consists mainly of traprock, which makes for tricky footing.

Bushwhack approach to bottom: Proceed downhill on Black Rock Road for 0.2 mile to reach the lakefront parking area. From here bushwhack around the east shore of the lake for 0.2 mile. The gully will be on your left, where clear views of the cascade can be obtained.

61

WADSWORTH BIG FALLS

Location: South of Rockfall (Middlesex County), Wadsworth Falls State Park
Delorme Connecticut/Rhode Island Atlas and Gazetteer: p. 35, H16; **Estimated GPS:** 41°31.59'N; 72°41.83'W
Views: Nearly head-on, lateral
Aesthetics: Excellent
Characteristics: Rural, historic, scenic, large, broad

Accessibility: 0.05-mile walk
Degree of Difficulty: Easy
Information: Wadsworth Falls State Park, 860-566-2304; trail map available at www.ct.gov/dep/cwp /view.asp?a=2716&q=325274 or www.middletownplanning.com /documents/MdtnTrailGuide.pdf

DESCRIPTION: Wadsworth Big Falls is on the Coginchaug River—a medium-sized stream which rises near Bluff Head and, after joining with the Mettabesset River at the Cromwell Meadows Wildlife Management Area, flows into the Connecticut River north of Middletown. The waterfall, 25 feet high and nearly twice as wide, falls over columnar pillars of Hampden Basalt. Remains of an old dam provide a convenient walkway out to the top of the falls.

HISTORY: Wadsworth Big Falls is in Wadsworth Falls State Park, a 267-acre preserve given to the State of Connecticut in 1942 by the Rockfall Corporation, a not-for-profit organization. Clarence C. Wadsworth, a noted Middletown scholar and linguist, established the organization and spent 40 years of his life advocating for Wadsworth Big Falls' preservation; it is named after him.

Vestiges of an old textile mill can be seen at the site. Nearby the Simeon

Wadsworth Big Falls broadly spans the Coginchaug River.

North gun factory produced military pistols during the 19th century which featured interchangeable parts.

A fairly well-preserved sluiceway can be seen a short distance upstream from the waterfall, just above the northwest end of the bridge spanning the Coginchaug River. Here a large, bow-shaped stone dam impounds the stream, forcing most of the river through an artificial channel.

The river's name, *Coginchaug,* is Native American for "long swamp."

DIRECTIONS: From Durham (junction of CT 147 and CT 17) drive northwest on CT 147 (Middlefield Road). At 2.8 miles, CT 147 veers off to the left toward Baileyville. Stay straight on CT 157, heading northeast and shortly passing through Middlefield. At 4.4 miles from Durham, turn right onto Cherry Hill Road.

Approaching from southwest of Middletown (junction of CT 66 and CT 157), proceed southwest on CT 157 for 2.7 miles and turn left onto Cherry Hill Road, now heading east.

From either direction you will come to a large parking area for Wadsworth Falls State Park on your left in 0.1 mile.

Walk across an open field toward the river. When you reach Wadsworth Big Falls you can head out along the top of a wide stone wall to a railed overlook of the falls, or walk down a flight of steps for lateral and near head-on views.

62

WADSWORTH LITTLE FALLS

Location: South of Rockfall (Middlesex County), Wadsworth Falls State Park
Delorme Connecticut/Rhode Island Atlas and Gazetteer: p. 35, H16; **Estimated GPS:** 41°31.59'N; 72°41.83'W
Views: Head-on, lateral
Aesthetics: Good

Characteristics: Remote, seasonal, tall
Accessibility: 0.5-mile hike
Degree of Difficulty: Top of cascade—moderately easy; base of cascade—moderately difficult
Information: Trail map available at http://www.ct.gov/dep/lib/dep /stateparks/maps/wadsworth.pdf

DESCRIPTION: Wadsworth Little Falls is on Wadsworth Brook—a tiny tributary to the Coginchaug River which rises in Wadsworth Falls State Park. The waterfall consists of a series of steplike drops, none individually greater than 3–4 feet in height, but which collectively form a 40-foot-high staircase of falling water.

Due to the stream's limited watershed, it's best to visit in the early spring or following heavy rainfall when more water is flowing.

DIRECTIONS: Follow the directions given to reach the parking area for Wadsworth Big Falls.

From the Wadsworth Big Falls parking area head east along Cherry Hill Road, crossing over a bridge spanning the Coginchaug River, and then over a set of railroad tracks. Several hundred feet beyond, you will come to the trailhead for Wadsworth Little Falls on your left. Follow the orange-blazed path (an old road) for 0.4 mile. When you come to two large wooden posts jutting up from the road, bear left, and follow a short, secondary path for 100 feet to the top of the cascade.

A side path leads down to the bottom of the falls, but the trail is quite steep, making good hiking shoes a requirement for this descent.

Wadsworth Little Falls—tall, slender, and seasonal

63

See page 216 for hiking map

SPRUCE GLEN FALLS

Location: North of Wallingford (New Haven County), Spruce Glen
Delorme Connecticut/Rhode Island Atlas and Gazetteer: p. 34, J10; **Estimated GPS:** 41°29.63'N; 72°47.80'W
Views: Lateral
Aesthetics: Good

Characteristics: Remote, scenic, small
Accessibility: 1.4-mile hike
Degree of Difficulty: Moderately difficult
Information: Trail map available at www.alcasoft.com/wlt/documents /TrailGuide.pdf

DESCRIPTION: Spruce Glen Falls is a 13-foot-high waterfall on Spruce Glen Brook—a small stream which rises south of Meriden and flows into Meetinghouse Brook just west of CT 15. The waterfall cuts the ravine deeply, permitting distant, trailside views of the falls.

Less than 0.2 mile further upstream is an old cement bridge where a sluiceway channels a short section of the stream. Just upstream from the sluiceway is a breached dam, with a small cascade at its west end. You may have passed over this cement bridge on the way up to the falls. Years ago the old bridge was part of a roadway that connected Tankwood Road to what has become a rest area along CT 15.

The part of the gorge containing the waterfall is particularly rugged, having been cut both deep and narrow by Spruce Glen Brook; it extends for 0.4 mile.

HISTORY: Spruce Glen Falls and Spruce Glen are overseen by the The Wallingford Land Trust, Inc. an organization which currently manages 14 properties encompassing over 200 acres. Boy Scout Troop Four cleared the trail to the falls, which passes through Orchard Glen and Spruce Glen, as an Eagle Scout project under the leadership of Eagle Scout Joe McLaughlin. The Spruce Glen portion contains 68 acres.

Part of the trail is dedicated to Charlie Uznanski, a longtime volunteer who died in 2012.

DIRECTIONS: Driving along CT 15 between Wallingford and Meriden, get off at exit 66 and turn left onto North Colony Road (US 5), heading south for 0.3 mile. Then turn left onto CT 68 and proceed east for 0.8 mile. At the second traffic light turn left onto Barnes Road North and drive north for over 0.8 mile until you come to a cul-de-sac. Park in front of the

The hike to Spruce Glen Falls, long but rewarding

green sign for Orchard Glen, a preserve the Barnes Family and the FIP Corporation gave to the Wallingford Land Trust in 1988.

Driving along I-91 between Wallingford and Meriden, head west on CT 68 (Barnes Road) for 1.7 miles and then turn right at the traffic light onto Barnes Road North. Drive north for 0.8 mile and park at the cul-de-sac.

Follow the WLT (Wallingford Land Trust) blazed trail from the parking area. It quickly leads to the Orchard Glen Trail in 0.1 mile. Turn left here. (Note: This is a very well-marked trail system, with signs periodically affirming that you are on the waterfall trail.) Eventually you will reach an open area where high tension wires run east to west. You can either continue straight, or turn left and head downhill, initially paralleling the power lines. Either way will take you past Spruce Glen Falls since this section of the trail is a closed loop.

We will assume that you choose to continue going straight ahead. Eventually the trail turns left, becoming the Spruce Glen Trail as it follows the WLT markers. You will soon start hearing the incessant drone of automobile traffic in the background emanating from CT 15; it will grow louder as you head downhill. After rapidly reaching an old concrete bridge, look for a breached dam just upstream from the bridge, along with a 2-foot-high cascade formed at the dam's west end.

Spruce Glen Falls, further downstream from the cement bridge, is in a deeper, more recessed part of the gorge. Continue on the trail as it veers left and begins heading downstream. In less than another 0.2 mile you will come to the waterfall on your left. It is in a fairly steep part of the ravine.

On your return trek you may wish to take the Falling Waters Trail, which follows a tiny tributary to Spruce Glen Brook for a short distance and then returns to the main trail. There are a number of tiny cascades along this creek, but none that are large enough to be counted as a waterfall.

64

 See page 217 for hiking map

STAIR BROOK FALLS

Location: Southwest of Durham (near the border between Middlesex and New Haven Counties)
Delorme Connecticut/Rhode Island Atlas and Gazetteer: p. 26, B2; **Estimated GPS:** 41°25.78'N; 72°43.66'W
Views: Head-on
Aesthetics: Good
Characteristics: Remote, scenic, seasonal

Accessibility: 0.5-mile hike
Degree of Difficulty: Base— moderately easy; upper section view—very difficult
Information: Trail map available in Ann T. Colson (ed.), *Connecticut Walk Book: The Guide to the Blue-Blazed Hiking Trails of Western Connecticut* (19th ed.), (Connecticut Forest & Park Association, 2006), page 109.

DESCRIPTION: This 40-foot-high cascade, aka Totoket Mountain Falls, is on Stair Brook—a medium-sized stream which rises from a swampy area on the Totoket Mountain plateau and flows into Parmalee Brook.

Where Stair Brook cuts a pass through a 100-foot-high ridge is the fairly impressive cascade.

DIRECTIONS: From south of Durham (junction of CT 17 and CT 77), head southwest on CT 17 (New Haven Road) for 3.9 miles. Turn left onto Stage Coach Road and park to your right where the road veers left at 0.2 mile.

Proceeding on foot, follow the blue-blazed Mattabasset Trail for 0.5 mile as it climbs gradually but steadily uphill. By the time the trail reaches the level of the stream you should be able to see Stair Brook Falls in the distance towering behind a canopy of trees. As you get closer you will come to realize that only the upper part of the cascading stream is actually the waterfall. Cross over the stream to better view the cascade.

For those who are secure about their rock-scrambling abilities, it is possible to ascend the sloping field of talus to get a better view of the cascade's upper section, but this is not recommended.

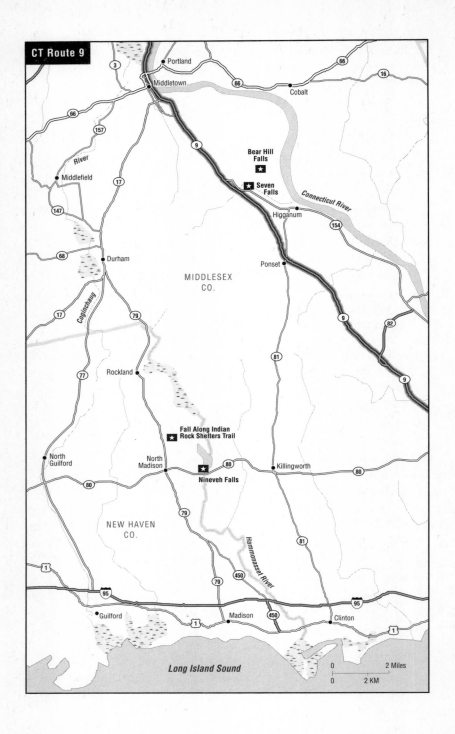

CT Route 9

Portland
3
Middletown
Cobalt
66
16
66
66
157
9
Bear Hill
Falls
★
River
Middlefield
17
★ Seven
Falls
Connecticut River
147
Higganum
154
68
Durham
Ponset
MIDDLESEX
CO.
Coginchaug
17
79
81
77
Rockland
82
9
Fall Along Indian
★ Rock Shelters Trail
North
Guilford
North
Madison
80
9
Killingworth
80
★
Nineveh Falls
80
NEW HAVEN
CO.
79
81
1
Hammonasset River
95
79
450
Guilford
1
Madison
450
Clinton
95
1

Long Island Sound

0   2 Miles
0   2 KM

FALLS ACCESSIBLE FROM CT 9

CT 9 starts off from New Britain, the state's highest city, and heads southeast to Old Saybrook, a medium-sized town located at the mouth of the Oyster River. After reaching Middletown, the highway parallels the Connecticut River.

65

BEAR HILL FALLS

Location: Northwest of Higganum (Middlesex County)
Delorme Connecticut/Rhode Island Atlas and Gazetteer: p. 35, H23; **Estimated GPS:** 41°30.85'N; 72°34.71'W
Views: Top—overlook; Bottom—head-on

Aesthetics: Fair/Good
Characteristics: Remote, scenic, medium-sized, seasonal
Accessibility: 0.5-mile hike
Degree of Difficulty: Moderate
Information: Trail map available at www.middletownplanning.com /documents/MdtnTrailGuide.pdf

DESCRIPTION: Bear Hill Falls is a 30-foot-high staircase cascade on the outlet stream from one of the three Asylum Reservoirs that flow into the Connecticut River north of Higganum. The Asylum Reservoirs were named because their alignment points in the direction of the Connecticut Valley Hospital. David Ellis, creator of the Connecticut Waterfalls Website, named the waterfall.

DIRECTIONS: Driving along CT 9 between Middletown and Higganum, get off at exit 10. Cross over Saybrook Road at the traffic light and proceed straight, going east on Aircraft Road for 0.8 mile. Pull over to your left when you see a blue-colored sign in front of the Mattabasset Trail. The trail to the falls begins across a short piece of private land owned by a utility company that graciously permits access to hikers.

Head north for 0.1 mile. When you come to a fork, bear right on the blue-blazed Mattabasset Trail. Note: The Bear Hill South Loop Trail leads left from the fork. Continue east along a ridgeline for nearly 0.4 mile. This is a dramatic part of the hike, for you will find yourself literally walking along an escarpment ledge with impressive drop-offs to your right. Some have called this the Chinese Wall, presumably after the Great Wall of China.

Bear Hill Falls, near the Asylum Reservoirs

At 0.5 mile from the start you will come to a stream which drops off the escarpment edge. Cross over it, keeping slightly back from the brink of the falls, and then scramble down the east bank for a view of the cascade from its base.

66

~~

SEVEN FALLS

Location: Northwest of Higganum (Middlesex County), Seven Falls State Park
Delorme Connecticut/Rhode Island Atlas and Gazetteer: p. 35, 123; **Estimated GPS:** 41°30.39'N; 72°34.81'W
Views: Head-on, lateral

Aesthetics: Fair/Good
Characteristics: Remote, small
Accessibility: Less than 0.05-mile walk
Degree of Difficulty: Easy
Information: Trail map available at www.middletownplanning.com /documents/MdtnTrailGuide.pdf

DESCRIPTION: Seven Falls is on Bible Rock Brook—a small stream which rises west of Cockaponset State Forest and flows into the Connecticut River by Higganum. The stream descends through a veritable rock garden of large boulders, producing a number of cascades over a total drop of 10 feet.

HISTORY: Bible Rock Brook was named for a curious, 18-foot-high rock formation further upstream whose giant slabs resemble an open book. The name Bible Rock first appeared on the Walling map of 1859.

Don't expect to see seven individual cascades at Seven Falls, for although *seven* rhymes with Heaven and seems fitting for a stream called Bible Rock Brook, you will be hard-pressed to count more than a couple of falls.

Seven Falls State Park was the first of what would become many rest-stop/picnic areas created in Connecticut, this one more heavily utilized in past days when Saybrook Road served as a main route to the shoreline.

DIRECTIONS: Driving along CT 9 between Middletown and Higganum, get off at exit 10. Turn right onto Saybrook Road (CT 154) and drive southeast for over 0.6 mile. As soon as you cross over Bible Rock Brook turn into a large pullout on your left. Two small cascades can be seen by looking upstream from the top of the Saybrook Road bridge.

Seven Falls, a series of tiny cascades formed on Bible Rock Brook

For good views of Seven Falls, walk down a short flight of stairs to a picnic area adjacent to the stream.

If you wish, you can continue across the bridge and follow the blue-blazed Mattabasset Trail east, heading downstream. It passes by the falls, initially paralleling Bible Rock Brook. After less than 0.1 mile, however, the trail suddenly veers left, following a tiny tributary for a short distance and leaving Bible Rock Brook behind.

67

NINEVEH FALLS

Location: West of Killingworth
(on the border between New
Haven and Middlesex Counties)
**Delorme Connecticut/Rhode
Island Atlas and Gazetteer:**
p. 26, F9; **Estimated GPS:**
41°21.43'N; 72°36.77'W
Views: Head-on

Aesthetics: Good
Characteristics: Remote, small,
huge dam looms at mouth of gorge
Accessibility: Less than 0.05-mile
walk
Degree of Difficulty: Moderately
easy

DESCRIPTION: Nineveh (also spelled Ninevah, Ninavah, and Nineyeh) Falls is on the Hammonasset River—a medium-sized stream which rises southeast of Durham and flows into Long Island Sound by Hammonasset Beach State Park.

The waterfall consists of 10 feet of drops and plunges surrounded by enormous boulders, all contained in a steeply cut gorge. Intimate views of the cascades are provided from a footbridge which crosses directly in front of the cascades.

The gorge ends several hundred feet upstream at an enormous dam which impounds Lake Hammonasset. Sources state that most of the original falls were destroyed when the reservoir was created.

Near the east end of the footbridge is a small, 4-foot-high cascade on a tiny tributary to the Hammonasset River.

A small stream flowing into the Hammonasset River near the southwest side of the CT 80 bridge produces several small cascades which can be seen by following the creek upstream for 50 feet.

HISTORY: Back in the 19th century the falls and gorge were a popular picnicking area and meeting place. It was also the site of several mills and a tannery.

According to an oft-repeated legend, the falls are haunted by the ghosts of a young, beautiful Native American maiden and her warrior brave. It is the familiar story of Romeo and Juliet, only now dressed up in Native American garb. The beautiful maiden, upon hearing that her betrothed was killed in battle, jumps off the high cliff to join him in death. The brave, however, is still alive, and returns to find that his bride-to-be is dead.

Nineveh Falls, located between a dam and a footbridge

Grieving inconsolably, he also takes his life at the falls—and it is their ghosts, united in death, that now haunt the site.

Built in the late 1940s and early 1950s, the dam's current name is the South Central Connecticut Regional Water Authority's dam.

DIRECTIONS: From North Madison (CT 79 and CT 80) drive east on CT 80 (Old Toll Road) for 1.3 miles. Park to your left just before crossing the bridge spanning the Hammonasset River.

From Killingworth (junction of CT 80 and CT 81), drive west on CT 80 for 2.7 miles. Park to your right as soon as you cross over the bridge. Be sure not to block the gated emergency entrance. Maintained as a public water supply, activities in the area are limited to hiking only.

From the parking area walk over to the northwest end of the bridge and follow a flight of stone steps that lead down along the side of the bridge to an attractive footbridge which spans the Hammonasset River immediately downstream from the falls.

68

∽

FALLS ALONG INDIAN ROCK SHELTERS TRAIL

Location: North of North Madison (New Haven County), Indian Rock Shelters **Delorme Connecticut/Rhode Island Atlas and Gazetteer:** p. 26, E7; **Estimated GPS:** 41°19.43'N; 72°35.60'W **Views:** Head-on **Aesthetics:** Fair **Characteristics:** Small, seasonal, near archaeologically significant location **Accessibility:** 1.2-mile hike (round-trip loop) **Degree of Difficulty:** Moderate **Information:** Trail map available at www.madisonlandtrust.com /wp-content/uploads/2011/10/Indian RockShelters.pdf

DESCRIPTION: This small, 6-foot-high cascade, consisting of two ledge drops, is near the top of an extensive 40- to 50-foot-high escarpment ridge.

HISTORY: The cascade is near two natural rock shelters that have formed along an impressive 1.0-mile-long escarpment wall. Archaeologists believe that the two cavities, each roughly 25 feet long, 7 feet high, and 8 feet deep, were used by the Hammonassett during the winter for shelter.

The Madison Land Conservation Trust manages the property.

DIRECTIONS: From North Madison (junction of CT 80 and CT 79), drive east on CT 80 for 0.8 mile. Turn left onto Summer Hill Road and proceed north for 0.7 mile. When you come to Twilight Drive, turn left, go 0.1 mile, and then turn right. After another 0.2 mile, turn right onto Lake Drive, and follow it for 0.3 mile to a cul-de-sac.

From here, take the blue-blazed, 1.2-mile-long Indian Rock Shelters Trail (a loop), going either clockwise or counterclockwise. The cascade is between the two Indian rock shelters.

Grayville Falls, Amston, Grayville Falls Town Park

Part II: Eastern Connecticut

There are five counties covered in this section:

Hartford County
Middlesex County
Tolland County
Windham County
New London County
For more information on each county, see page XXIX.

FALLS ACCESSIBLE FROM I-91

I-91 enters Connecticut near Longmeadow, Massachusetts, and follows along the Connecticut River, switching over to the river's west side at Windsor Locks (see Western Connecticut section for waterfalls near I-91 in that area).

69

SCANTIC RAPIDS

Location: South of Hazardville (Hartford County)
Delorme Connecticut/Rhode Island Atlas and Gazetteer: p. 54, E1; **Estimated GPS:** 41°58.90'N; 73°32.38'W
Views: Head-on, lateral
Aesthetics: Good

Characteristics: Urban, scenic, small
Accessibility: Less than 0.05-mile walk
Degree of Difficulty: Easy
Information: Enfield Historical Society, 860-745-1729

DESCRIPTION: These small cascades and rapids are formed on the Scantic River—a medium-sized river that rises from Tray Hollow and Culver Pond in the Stafford swamps, and flows into the Connecticut River near East Windsor Hill.

Although none of the cascades are much larger than large rapids, the south bank of the river gives a striking view of the totality of water falling over nearly 0.05 mile.

On the side of the river opposite from the parking lot is a pump station next to an old ruin. The bridge, rebuilt in 2010, overlooks the river.

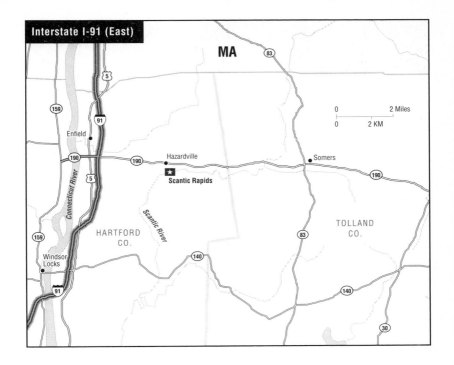

HISTORY: The name of the river, Scantic, comes from the Scantuck, a tribe of Native Americans who once lived in the region. Every year the rapids are part of the annual Scantic Spring Splash, an event held for white-water paddlers.

Hazardville is historically known for its production of gunpowder. It all began in 1836 when Loomis, Denslow, and Company erected a gunpow-der mill. In 1837 Colonel Agustus G. Hazard acquired 1/4 interest in the company and by 1843 was its principal owner. The company expanded fur-ther in 1854 when a competing gunpowder factory was taken over and incorporated into the business. During the Civil War the powder company supplied the Union Army with much of its gunpowder.

A terrible accident in 1913 destroyed the factory and ended production for good. Some foundation walls which survived are still visible today.

DIRECTIONS: From I-91 get off at exit 47 (east) for Hazardville and proceed east on CT 190 (Hazard Avenue) for approximately 2.5 miles. Turn right onto South Maple Street, opposite where CT 192 comes in on the left, and drive south for 0.3 mile.

As soon as you cross over the bridge spanning the Scantic River, turn

The Scantic Rapids will carry you away.

left into a large parking area. The tiny cascades and rapids are visible head-on from the top of the bridge, or laterally from along the south bank of the river.

FALLS ACCESSIBLE FROM CT 2

CT 2 begins east of Hartford, initially paralleling the Connecticut River until reaching Glastonbury. At that point CT 2 pulls away dramatically from the Connecticut River, continuing its southeast run as it cuts across the state diagonally, veering east at Colchester to its terminus at Norwich.

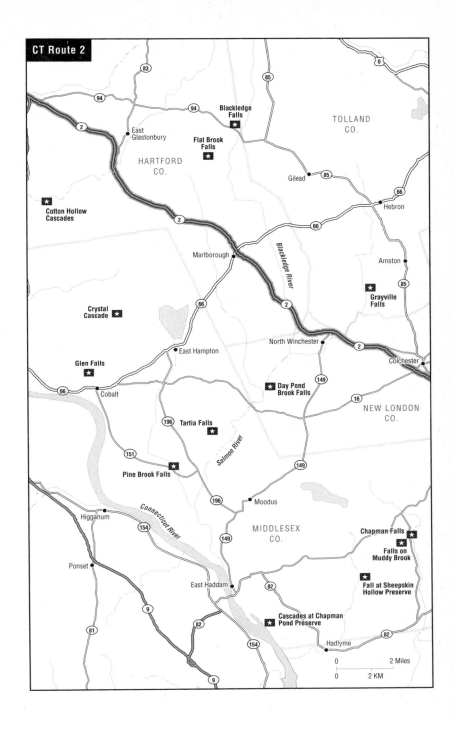

CT Route 2

★ Cotton Hollow Cascades

East Glastonbury

HARTFORD CO.

Blackledge Falls ★

Flat Brook Falls ★

TOLLAND CO.

Gilead

Hebron

Amston

Marlborough

Blackledge River

Crystal Cascade ★

Grayville Falls ★

Glen Falls ★

East Hampton

North Winchester

Colchester

Cobalt

Day Pond Brook Falls ★

NEW LONDON CO.

Tartia Falls ★

Salmon River

Pine Brook Falls ★

Moodus

Higganum

MIDDLESEX CO.

Chapman Falls ★

Falls on Muddy Brook ★

Ponset

Connecticut River

East Haddam

Fall at Sheepskin Hollow Preserve ★

Cascades at Chapman Pond Preserve ★

Hadlyme

0   2 Miles

0   2 KM

70

COTTON HOLLOW CASCADES

Location: South Glastonbury (Hartford County), Cotton Hollow Nature Preserve
Delorme Connecticut/Rhode Island Atlas and Gazetteer: p. 44, L10; **Estimated GPS:** Upper—41°39.88'N; 72°35.02'W; Lower—41°39.90'N; 72°36.21'W
Views: Head-on, lateral
Aesthetics: Good
Characteristics: Rural, scenic, small

Accessibility: Main falls—0.05-mile walk; end of North Trail—0.5-mile hike; descent into gorge from Tree Trail—0.3-mile hike
Degree of Difficulty: Main falls—easy; downstream into gorge—moderately difficult
Information: Town of Glastonbury, 860-652-7710

DESCRIPTION: The 8-foot-high cascade at the east end of Cotton Hollow is on Roaring Brook—a medium-sized stream which rises southeast of Manchester and flows into the Connecticut River west of South Glastonbury. A breached dam can be seen at the top of the cascade. This area is open to the public from the third Saturday of April to June 15th; at all other times access is limited to residents of Glastonbury only.

Entering the side of the cascade from the north is a tiny tributary which produces several miniature cascades of its own. A number of small cascades and chutes have formed in the hollow at various distances downstream from the main cascade.

HISTORY: The 83-acre Cotton Hollow Nature Preserve is the site of a number of 18th and 19th century sawmills, gristmills, iron foundries, and a cotton mill. The cotton mill, the hollow's namesake, was built in 1814. Its ruins are still visible today.

DIRECTIONS: Driving along CT 2 south of East Glastonbury, get off at exit 10. Go south on Manchester Road (CT 83) for roughly 0.15 mile. Turn right onto New London Turnpike and head northwest for 0.6 mile. When you come to Chestnut Hill Road, turn left and drive west for 0.8 mile. Then turn left onto Hopewell Road and proceed southwest for 1.6 miles. The parking area for the Cotton Hollow Nature Preserve is on your left.

From east of Portland (junction of CT 66 and CT 17) drive north on CT 17 for 6.8 miles. At a traffic light turn right onto Hopewell Road and

Past industries in Cotton Hollow were heavily dependent on Roaring Brook for hydropower.

proceed east for 1.2 miles. The parking area for the Cotton Hollow Nature Preserve is on your right.

From the east end of the parking area take the blue/white-blazed North Trail downhill for 100 feet until you reach a boulder with a plaque on it honoring the late Eric Carl Schluntz, a Glastonbury resident and fisheries biologist. Turn left off the main trail, and follow an unmarked trail upstream along the north bank for less than 0.05 mile to the main cascade, which lies virtually downhill from the town's swimming pool. You will pass by old stone foundations to the right of the trail and foundations next to the falls.

Return to the junction and follow the blue/white-blazed North Trail downstream through the east section of Cotton Hollow. In 0.3 mile you will come to an area where the gorge narrows significantly, forming a 2- to 3-foot-high cascade. The stream then runs through a 30-foot-long flume into a large shallow pool and exits over a 1- to 2-foot-high cascade formed by a row of three large boulders. This is a rugged area abounding with massive boulders.

From here, the trail continues downstream for less than 0.2 mile farther. Several small cascades are passed, with the hiking becoming considerably more demanding.

Lower end of Cotton Hollow: If you wish, the lower section of Cotton

Hollow can be accessed from its west end. From the junction of Hopewell Road and CT 17 (Main Street), drive south on CT 17 for 0.2 mile, cross over Roaring Brook, and then turn immediately left at the South Tavern. The parking area for Cotton Hollow Nature Preserve is behind the tavern near the northeast corner.

Follow the Tree Trail east upstream for 0.3 mile, passing by rapids and old foundations of houses where mill workers once lived. Turn left at a side path that leads steeply down to the river, ending up at a massive, 8-foot-thick breached stone dam. Across the river can be seen the still intact 4-story-high ruins of a former paper mill. Small cascades are visible further upstream where the gorge becomes rocky and dissected.

71

BLACKLEDGE FALLS

Location: East of East Glastonbury (Hartford County)
Delorme Connecticut/Rhode Island Atlas and Gazetteer: p. 45, J18; **Estimated GPS:** 41°41.86'N; 72°27.35'W
Views: Head-on
Aesthetics: Good
Accessibility: 0.4-mile hike

Characteristics: Remote, medium-sized, seasonal
Degree of Difficulty: Moderate
Information: Glastonbury Parks and Recreation Department, 860-652-7679; trail map available at http://www.glasct.org/Modules/Show Document.aspx?documentid=4777

DESCRIPTION: Blackledge Falls is on a small tributary to the Blackledge River. The tributary rises from a pond on the east shoulder of 895-foot-high John Tom Hill, and flows into Blackledge Brook Pond, which is part of the Blackledge River system.

Blackledge Falls consists of a central 20-foot-high waterfall which drops over a wide cliff of bedrock; 20 feet to the right is a second waterfall, virtually as high but receiving less water from the stream. Under heavy flow, a third waterfall, to the left of the main falls, often appears.

HISTORY: Blackledge Falls is in a 79-acre parcel of land abutting Gay City State Park to the north. The town of Glastonbury owns and manages the park, which was dedicated in 1991.

In his 1675 will, Joshua, third son of Uncas, called the Blackledge River *unguoshot*—Native American for "land at the bend, or crotch, of the brook,"

Blackledge Falls, contained in its own park

a fitting description of the enormous eastward bend in the river at its junction with Fawn Brook.

The name Blackledge is attributable to John Blackleach, a contemporary of Joshua, who paid taxes on the land in the Five Mile Purchase of 1673.

DIRECTIONS: From CT 2 get off at exit 10 for East Glastonbury and drive north on CT 83 (Manchester Road) for roughly 2.6 miles. When you come to the junction of CT 94 and CT 83, turn right onto CT 94 (Hebron Avenue) and head east for 4.1 miles. Turn left into a paved parking area by the Blackledge Falls sign.

From Hebron (junction of CT 66 and CT 85), drive northwest on CT 85 for 4.8 miles. Then turn left onto CT 94 and proceed west for 1.2 miles. The Blackledge Falls parking area is on your right.

Follow the blue/white-blazed trail northwest for 0.4 mile to the falls. The trail initially takes you past the west shore of Blackledge Brook Pond, and then gradually uphill to the waterfall. Pay attention to the trail markers, for at one point you will come to a junction where a blue-blazed trail heads right. Continue left on the blue/white-blazed trail.

A kiosk next to the parking lot shows the configuration of trails in the park. Take note that the hike up to the falls can be shortened by taking a connecting trail northwest from the parking lot; however, if you do this, you won't get to see Blackledge Brook Pond along the way.

72

See page 217 for hiking map

FLAT BROOK FALLS

Location: South of East Glastonbury (Hartford County)
Delorme Connecticut/Rhode Island Atlas and Gazetteer: p. 45, J17; **Estimated GPS:** 41°41.60'N; 72°28.40'W
Views: Head-on
Aesthetics: Good
Characteristics: Remote, scenic, medium-sized, seasonal

Accessibility: 0.7-mile hike
Degree of Difficulty: Moderate
Information: Trail map available in Ann T. Colson (ed.), *Connecticut Walk Book: The Guide to the Blue-Blazed Hiking Trails of Eastern Connecticut* (19th ed.), (Connecticut Forest & Park Association, 2006), page 134.

DESCRIPTION: This small, 20-foot-high cascade is on a tiny tributary to

Flat Brook which rises in the hills south of Diamond Lake. Flat Brook is a small stream from Diamond Lake flowing into the Blackledge River a short distance downstream from Flat Brook Falls.

The hike follows a short section of the Shenipsit Trail—a 41-mile-long path which extends from East Hampton to within 3.0 miles of the Massachusetts border. *Shenipsit* is Native American for "at the great pool."

Nearby Diamond Lake is privately owned and surrounded by an area that continues to be subdivided into high-end residential homes.

DIRECTIONS: From CT 2, near Marlborough, get off at exit 13 and head south on Hebron Road (CT 66) for roughly 0.2 mile. Turn right onto North Main Street, and then, in 0.05 mile, right again onto Jones Hollow Road. Head north for 3.1 miles, then bear left at a fork onto Finley/Marlborough Road and continue north for another 1.2 miles until you reach Imperial Drive, on your left.

Approaching from north of East Glastonbury (junction of CT 94 and CT 83), drive east on CT 94 (Hebron Avenue) for 3.0 miles. Turn right onto Marlborough Road and drive south for 0.7 mile to Imperial Drive, on your right.

Coming from either direction, turn west onto Imperial Drive. Drive 0.05

Flat Brook Falls—an oasis of beauty surrounded by suburbia

mile, turn left onto Empress Lane, and park immediately to the side of the road so that you are not close to any of the private residences.

Walk down the sidewalk along Imperial Drive for 0.1 mile to reach the point where the Shenipsit Trail crosses the road, 0.2 mile from Marlborough Road. Turn left and follow the aqua-blazed Shenipsit Trail south for 0.5 mile. For much of the hike you will be walking along the sloping west bank of the ravine, with the stream to your left. At 0.4 mile you will cross over a small but pretty tributary to Flat Brook. Continue south on the aqua-blazed trail for another 0.1 mile. When the aqua-blazed trail turns right and begins climbing uphill, continue to your left on a white-blazed side trail which takes you down and across Flat Creek in a couple of hundred feet. You have just arrived at an enchanting place enclosed by evergreens, complete with a fire ring and stone slabs with back supports for sitting. Directly across the stream, a small tributary to Flat Creek produces a 20-foot-high cascade.

73

See page 218 for hiking map

CRYSTAL CASCADE

Location: East of Portland (Middlesex County)
Delorme Connecticut/Rhode Island Atlas and Gazetteer: p. 36, C1; **Estimated GPS:** 41°35.58'N; 72°32.61'W
Views: Head-on
Aesthetics: Good
Characteristics: Remote, scenic, medium-sized

Accessibility: 0.8-mile hike
Degree of Difficulty: Moderately difficult
Information: Trail map available in Ann T. Colson (ed.), *Connecticut Walk Book: The Guide to the Blue-Blazed Hiking Trails of Eastern Connecticut* (19th ed.), (Connecticut Forest & Park Association, 2006), page 130.

DESCRIPTION: Crystal Cascade, aka The Cascades, is a 20-foot-high waterfall on Carr Brook—a small stream whose south branch rises from a swampy area east of the Bald Hill Range and flows into the Connecticut River near Gildersleeve. Moss covers the surface of Crystal Cascade, giving it a slick, slippery appearance. The base includes a small pool of water.

HISTORY: Crystal Cascade is in the Meshomasic State Forest, the first

Crystal Cascade, along the Shenipsit Trail

woods to be designated a state forest in Connecticut (and the second to be designated a state forest in the United States).

DIRECTIONS: From Glastonbury (junction of CT 17 and CT 2), drive south on CT 17 for roughly 8.0 miles. When you reach the junction of CT 17 and CT 17A, continue south on CT 17 for another 0.3 mile and then turn left onto Cox Road.

From east of Portland (junction of CT 66 and CT 17), head north on CT 17 for 1.7 miles and turn right onto Cox Road.

Approaching from either direction, proceed east on Cox Road for 0.4 mile. Then turn left onto Rose Hill Road and, after 100 feet, turn right, back onto Cox Road. Continue east on Cox Road (not resetting the odometer). At nearly 1.9 miles you will cross over Great Hill Road. Continue straight ahead on Cox Road for another 0.7 mile (or a total of 2.6 miles from CT 17). Then turn right onto Wood Chopper Road/Gadpouch Road (a dirt road with no sign) and head east for 1.4 miles. Look for where the Shenipsit Trail crosses Wood Chopper Road. Park in a small area to your left.

The hike to Crystal Cascade involves a 0.8-mile hike along a section of the blue-blazed Shenipsit Trail. From the parking area, proceed north for 0.2 mile. When you come to a *T* turn left, quickly passing by an old quarry on your right. After 0.3 mile you will see a blue painted arrow on a tree directing you to turn left. Continue on the blue-blazed Shenipsit Trail for another 0.3 mile. You will soon come to Carr Brook and then down to the top of the cascade. The trail crosses the stream here. Be sure that you cross far enough back from the cascade so as not to slip and accidentally go over the top. In another 100 feet you will reach the bottom of the cascade, where there are excellent head-on views.

74

GRAYVILLE FALLS

Location: Amston (Tolland County), Grayville Falls Town Park
Delorme Connecticut/Rhode Island Atlas and Gazetteer: p. 36, C11; **Estimated GPS:** Air Line Trail—41°36.86'N; 72°21.40'W; Grayville Falls Town Park—41°36.83'N; 72°22.14'W
Views: Lateral
Aesthetics: Fair

Characteristics: Remote, small, a long waterslide
Accessibility: 0.1-mile walk
Degree of Difficulty: Moderately easy
Information: Trail map (of Air Line Trail) available at www.ct.gov /dep/lib/dep/greenways/airlinetrail brochure.pdf

DESCRIPTION: Grayville Falls is a 10-foot-high, impressively long natural waterslide on Raymond Brook—a small stream which rises from a lake northeast of Hebron and flows into Jenny Brook. It is the totality of falling water along the tilted, terraced streambed that captivates the eye—not any particular individual, tiny cascade.

A breached dam can be seen at the top of the waterslide. Just upstream, a tall footbridge crosses from one side of the stream to the other.

HISTORY: Grayville Falls is at Grayville Falls Town Park, established by the town of Hebron in 1971. The park was named after the William Gray Carpet Warp Manufacturing Company, whose ruins can be seen near the falls.

Hebron's name has biblical roots going back to Hebron, a city closely associated with King David in the Bible.

The Air Line State Park Trail, which runs in close proximity to the Grayville Falls Town Park, begins in East Hampton and ends in Putnam 50 miles later.

DIRECTIONS: From CT 2, get off at exit 13 for Marlborough. Head northeast on CT 66 (Hebron Road) for roughly 5.2 miles to Hebron.

From Hebron (junction of CT 66 and CT 85), proceed south on CT 85 (Colchester Road/Church Street) for 1.4 miles. As CT 85 veers left, continue straight ahead (south) on Old Colchester Road for another 1.9 miles. When you come to Grayville Road turn right. From here it is 0.4 mile to where the road crosses the Air Line State Park Trail and 0.6 mile to the

Grayville Falls—one long, continuous waterslide

left-hand entrance to Grayville Falls Town Park, opposite O'Reidy Road. Use of the Grayville Falls Town Park facilities is limited to residents of Hebron.

To waterslide from Air Line State Park Trail: Walk south for 0.05 mile and then take a side path on your right that leads down quickly to Raymond Brook, only several hundred feet away. Grayville Falls is directly downstream from the footbridge and breached dam.

To waterslide from Grayville Falls Town Park: From the parking lot, walk east across an open field toward the woods guided by the sound of the waterfall, which is only several hundred feet away.

75

See page 218 for hiking map

DAY POND BROOK FALLS

Location: North Westchester (New London County), Day Pond State Park
Delorme Connecticut/Rhode Island Atlas and Gazetteer: p. 36, F8; **Estimated GPS:** 41°33.50'N; 72°25.22'W
Views: Head-on, lateral

Aesthetics: Excellent
Characteristics: Remote, scenic, medium-sized
Accessibility: 1.0-mile hike
Degree of Difficulty: Moderate
Information: Trail map available at www.ct.gov/dep/lib/dep/stateparks/maps/daypond.pdf

DESCRIPTION: Day Pond Brook Falls is a multitiered, 25-foot-high cascade on the outlet stream from Day Pond, which flows into the Salmon River 0.2 mile downstream from the falls. Just before the main falls is a 5-foot-high cascade.

HISTORY: The stone foundation ruins of an old sawmill, its sluiceway, and the stone-lined rectangular pit that once housed an overshot water-

Day Pond Brook Falls on a tributary to the Salmon River

wheel, are located a few hundred feet from the falls. Day Pond State Park was created in 1949.

DIRECTIONS: Driving along CT 2, get off at exit 16 for North Westchester and proceed south on CT 149 for about 3.0 miles. Make a hard right turn onto Peck Lane and head north for over 0.1 mile. When you come to Day Pond Road turn left and drive west for 0.2 mile. Then turn right into Day Pond State Park, go 0.3 mile, and park in an area near the end of the road.

From the parking area, proceed across the outlet dam, past a kiosk, and over to where Day Pond Road continues as a footpath. (Note: The longer Salmon River Trail/South Loop, off Day Pond Road, will also get you to the falls, passing by an enormous glacial boulder along the way.) Walk northwest along this old road for 0.7 mile until you reach a blue-blazed trail that comes in on your left (the upper part of the Salmon River Trail/South Loop). Follow it for 75 feet, and then take the clearly marked Day Pond Falls Spur Trail to your right for 0.2 mile to the cascade.

76

TARTIA FALLS

Location: East of Middle Hampton (Middlesex County)
Delorme Connecticut/Rhode Island Atlas and Gazetteer: p. 36, G5; **Estimated GPS:** 42°32.39'N; 72°28.55'W
Views: Head-on

Aesthetics: Good
Characteristics: Rural, historic, medium-sized
Accessibility: Lower falls—roadside; upper falls—0.2-mile hike
Degree of Difficulty: Upper falls—moderately easy

DESCRIPTION: 25-foot-high Tartia Falls, aka Engel Falls, consists of a series of drops that continue down to the Tartia Road bridge. The waterfall is on Safstrom Brook—a small stream which rises in the hills southeast of East Hampton, and flows into the Salmon River near Wopowog. Large slabs of rock and boulders lie strewn about, giving the impression that the site was once quarried.

Near the top of the waterfall are the remains of an old stone dam that once impounded Safstrom Brook.

Tartia Falls, one of the prettiest roadside waterfalls in Connecticut

Roughly 0.2 mile further upstream a 7-foot-high, moss-covered cascade flows into a languid pool of water.

HISTORY: Two 7-foot-high stone pillars, virtually at roadside, are all that remain of a cider mill that once utilized the falls for hydropower.

To the right of the hill is a small artificial cave where cider produced by the mill was kept cool.

DIRECTIONS: From CT 2 get off at exit 13 for Marlborough. Proceed southwest on CT 66 for roughly 4.1 miles to East Hampton and then turn left onto CT 196 (Main Street). Drive south for 1.6 miles until you come to the junction with CT 16 (Colchester Avenue), south of East Hampton.

Turn left onto CT 16 and head east for 1.9 miles. Then turn right onto Tartia Road and go south for 2.0 miles until you come to a small bridge spanning Safstrom Brook. Tartia Falls is on the right, upstream from the bridge, and best seen from the roadside.

The upper falls can be accessed by following a path upstream along the north bank for less than 0.2 mile. To access the upper falls, private property must be crossed. Only do so if not posted.

77

PINE BROOK FALLS

Location: South of East Hampton (Middlesex County)
Delorme Connecticut/Rhode Island Atlas and Gazetteer: p. 36, H4; **Estimated GPS:** 41°31.26'N; 72°30.20'W
Views: Head-on, lateral
Aesthetics: Good
Characteristics: Remote, historic, scenic, small,

Accessibility: 0.3-mile hike
Degree of Difficulty: Moderately easy
Information: Middlesex Land Trust, 860-343-7537; information (but no trail map) available at www.middlesexlandtrust.org/word press/?P=166

DESCRIPTION: Pine Brook Falls consists of a series of small cascades on Pine Brook—a medium-sized stream which rises from the southwest edge of the Meshomasic State Forest west of East Hampton (where it is called the Green River), and flows into the Salmon River southwest of Moodus, cutting out a fairly deep ravine as it reaches the Salmon River.

Pine Brook Falls, once the site of much industrial activity

The remains of a massive stone dam span the top of an 8-foot-high upper falls. From here the stream passes through a shallow, rocky gorge, producing a number of smaller cascades within a span of several hundred feet.

HISTORY: Pine Brook Falls is part of a 40-acre preserve in the southeast section of East Hampton. In 2003 the Nature Conservancy, in conjunction with the Middlesex Land Trust, acquired the land from Richard and Sally Haase (who had owned the parcel since 1969), with the stipulation that it be transferred to the Middlesex Land Trust for 1/4 the purchase price, which it was. In 2011 the Middlesex Land Trust sold the property to the U.S. Fish and Wildlife Service. It is now part of the expanding Salmon River Division of the Silvio O. Conte National Fish and Wildlife Refuge.

Unlike nearby Moodus Falls, which is below the Moodus Reservoir and off-limits to the public, Pine Brook Falls remains accessible thanks to the combined efforts of private individuals and conservation/preservation groups.

DIRECTIONS: From northwest of Moodus (junction of CT 151 and CT 196), drive west on CT 151 for 1.1 miles. Turn right onto Sexton Hill Road and head downhill, going north, for 0.1 mile. Pull into a small parking area on your left before crossing over Pine Brook.

Walk around the barricade and follow an old mill road that leads to the falls in less than 0.3 mile.

78

See page 219 for hiking map

GLEN FALLS

Location: Cobalt (Middlesex County), Okumsett Preserve **Delorme Connecticut/Rhode Island Atlas and Gazetteer:** p. 35, F24; **Estimated GPS:** 41°33.91'N; 72°33.52'W
Views: Head-on from a distance

Aesthetics: Good
Characteristics: Remote, scenic, medium-sized
Accessibility: 0.3-mile hike
Degree of Difficulty: Moderately easy

DESCRIPTION: Glen Falls is a 20-foot-high waterfall on Great Hills Pond Brook, aka Cobalt Stream—the outlet creek from Great Hills Pond, which flows into the Connecticut River south of Cobalt. The brook was named for its association with Great Hills Pond and the towering Great Hill which overlooks the east side of the pond.

The cascade falls nearly vertically over a massive wall of bedrock which wraps around the north end of the gorge.

HISTORY: The Middlesex Land Trust established the 6-acre Okumsett Preserve through sustained efforts.

Glen Falls—a hidden gem of a waterfall

An impressive keystone tunnel on the way to Glen Falls

A number of past industries used Great Hills Pond Brook for hydropower, including the Wells and Clark Brothers' gristmills, Tibbal and Company's sawmill, Oakum Works, Bailey Brothers' gristmills, J. C. Clark Bell Founder, and the coffin trimming and silver plating factory.

DIRECTIONS: From CT 2 get off at exit 13 for Marlborough, and proceed southwest on CT 66 for 7.6 miles to Cobalt (junction of CT 66 and CT 151). Turn right onto Depot Hill Road, head north for 0.1 mile, and then bear left onto Middle Haddam Road. In less than 0.1 mile, turn left onto Grist Mill Lane and park immediately to the side of the road.

From here, walk west on Middle Haddam Road for 100 feet, crossing over Great Hills Pond Brook. The trailhead starts from a barricade on your right, just past the stream. Follow the red-blazed trail north through the 6-acre Taylor Brook Preserve. In several hundred feet you will come to a 75-foot-long tunnel under the abandoned Airline railroad bed. This magnificent keystone-block structure, 25 feet tall and 30 feet wide, serves as a right-of-way between the Taylor Brook Preserve and the Okumsett Preserve.

Walk through the tunnel and continue following the red-blazed trail through the Okumsett Preserve for 0.2 mile to the falls. Although Glen Falls is on private land, it can be observed from the north border of the Okumsett Preserve. Along the way you will pass by a breached stone dam, a relic from past days when over a half dozen mills and factories used the stream for hydropower.

79

CASCADES AT CHAPMAN POND PRESERVE

Location: East Haddam (Middlesex County), Cynthia B. Carlson Nature Preserve
Delorme Connecticut/Rhode Island Atlas and Gazetteer: p. 27, A19; **Estimated GPS:** 41°26.76'N; 72°26.21'W
Views: Lateral
Aesthetics: Fair

Characteristics: Remote, scenic, small, seasonal
Accessibility: 0.9-mile hike
Degree of Difficulty: Moderately difficult
Information: Trail map available at www.ehlt.org/EHLT%20Chapman %20Pond%20Preserve%20Map.jpg

DESCRIPTION: Two small cascades are formed on a small tributary roughly 0.05 mile upstream from the southeast end of Chapman Pond. A 6-foot-high, elongated cascade is immediately followed by a 3-foot-high cascade. In themselves, the two cascades hardly merit a visit, but combined with Chapman Pond—a unique geological anomaly—they make for an interesting outing.

HISTORY: The Cynthia B. Carlson Nature Preserve encompasses over 700 acres of land and water abutting the Connecticut River. At one time the area consisted of a verdant flatland farmers harvested for tall grasses to feed their livestock. The flood of 1936 changed the topography of the land forever, transforming the grassy meadow into a large, 60-acre freshwater tidal pond connected to the Connecticut River by two tiny creeks.

The first piece of property in the Chapman Pond area consisted of 290 acres of land purchased by the Nature Conservancy from Vivian Kellum. From this starting point, additional acquisitions were subsequently made.

The preserve is named after Cynthia B. Carlson, a landowner and conservationist who fought a utility company's attempt to keep its unsightly power lines and towers above ground.

DIRECTIONS: From CT 2 get off at exit 13 for Marlborough and proceed southwest on CT 66 for 4.1 miles to East Hampton (junction of CT 66 and CT 196). Turn left onto CT 196 and drive south for 5.4 miles. When you come to CT 151, northwest of Moodus, head southeast on CT 151 for 5.5 miles to its junction with CT 82, northeast of East Haddam. Proceed straight ahead on CT 82 east, continuing southeast for 1.2 miles, and turn right onto River Road. Head southwest for over 0.3 mile. Then turn right onto a dirt road where River Road curves sharply left and drive 0.1 mile to the parking area for the Cynthia B. Carlson Nature Preserve.

The trail from the parking area leads immediately to a 3.0-mile-long loop trail. Follow the trail clockwise (going left), descending gradually for the next 0.7 mile. Eventually you will come to a stream in a deep gully to your right. After less than 0.1 mile the trail crosses the stream, where the abutments of a former bridge can be seen on your left. The cascades are directly below here.

After seeing the cascades hikers would be remiss not to continue along the trail for another 0.05 mile to reach Chapman Pond. The trail now follows along the east shoreline of the pond, providing superlative views of this unique body of water.

If you continue following the trail it will eventually loop back to the connecting trail from the parking area. Along the way, roughly 2.0 miles into the walk, you may catch a glimpse of a cascade several hundred feet from the trail on the small stream you have been following. It is not very high, and is beyond the conservation easement boundary.

ADDITIONAL CASCADE: A 10-foot-high staircase waterfall, formed on Succor Brook, is visible from the roadside on the way down to East Haddam. From the junction of CT 82 and CT 151, take CT 82 west (instead of going east toward Chapman Pond) for 0.7 mile. The waterfall is directly to your right before Porges Road (41°27.61'N; 72°27.43'W), upstream from the bridge spanning Succor Brook.

80

 See page 219 for hiking map

WATERFALL AT SHEEPSKIN HOLLOW PRESERVE

Location: East Haddam (Middlesex County), Sheepskin Hollow Preserve

Delorme Connecticut/Rhode Island Atlas and Gazetteer: p. 36, K11; **Estimated GPS:** 41°27.86'N; 72°22.33'W

Views: Head-on, lateral

Aesthetics: Good

Characteristics: Remote, scenic, medium-sized

Accessibility: 0.3-mile hike

Degree of Difficulty: Moderate

Information: Trail map available at www.ehlt.org/EHLT%20Sheepskin%20Hollow%20Preserve%20Map.jpg

DESCRIPTION: This two-tiered, 25-foot-high waterfall is on Roaring Brook—a medium-sized stream which rises northeast of Mt. Parnassus and flows into the Connecticut River at Whalebone Cove, west of Hadlyme.

At the upper tier the stream drops 10 feet, partially emerging from a shelter cave at the bottom of the cascade. The stream immediately goes over a second drop, formed by 15 feet of cascades.

HISTORY: The 96-acre Sheepskin Hollow Preserve is part of the East Haddam Land Trust. The preserve's name harkens back to the time during the 18th and 19th centuries when local farmers raised sheep and operated tanneries.

DIRECTIONS: From CT 2 get off at exit 13 for Marlborough and proceed southwest on CT 66 for 4.1 miles to East Hampton (junction of CT 66 and CT 196). Turn left onto CT 196 and drive south for 5.4 miles. When you come to CT 151, northwest of Moodus, head southeast on CT 151 for 5.5 miles to the junction with CT 82, northeast of East Haddam. Continue straight on CT 82 east for a couple hundred feet, and then turn left onto Parnassus Road, proceeding east for 3.5 miles. Turn right onto Warner Road and go southeast for 0.6 mile. When you come to Ridgebury Road, turn right and head south for 0.2 mile until you reach a cul-de-sac at the end of a residential section. Be sure not to block anyone's driveway when you park.

Look for a marked trailhead between two houses where a sign states HIKING ONLY. From the cul-de-sac follow the white-blazed trail south for less than 0.05 mile. Turn left onto the yellow-blazed trail, follow it downhill to Roaring Brook, and then cross over a footbridge to the opposite side (a distance of 0.1 mile from the white-blazed trail). As soon as you start uphill turn right onto the blue-blazed trail and follow it southwest, paralleling the south bank of Roaring Brook. Within 0.1 mile you will come to a scenic rocky gorge and then, after another 100 feet, to the top of a 25-foot-high waterfall. A side path leads down to the base of the cascade.

81

CHAPMAN FALLS

Location: Northeast of East Haddam (Middlesex County), Devils Hopyard State Park
Delorme Connecticut/Rhode Island Atlas and Gazetteer: p. 37, K13; **Estimated GPS:** 41°29.08'N; 72°20.53'W
Views: Head-on, lateral
Aesthetics: Excellent
Characteristics: Remote, scenic, robust, large

Accessibility: 0.05-mile walk
Degree of Difficulty: Side of descending walkway—easy; side path leading down to base of falls—moderate
Information: Devils Hopyard State Park, 860-873-8566; trail map available at /www.ct.gov /dep/lib/dep/stateparks/maps /devilshopyard.pdf

DESCRIPTION: Chapman Falls is a three-tiered, 60-foot-high waterfall on the Eightmile River—a medium-sized stream which rises from a tiny lake northwest of the park and flows into the Connecticut River northeast of Essex. Adding to the attractiveness of the falls is the large pool of water at its base.

The surrounding bedrock, a feature which is almost as eye-catching as the waterfall itself, is made out of Scotland Schist.

At times, a tiny stream which emerges from the Hopyard Road tunnel produces a series of tiny cascades on its way down to the base of Chapman Falls.

HISTORY: Chapman Falls is in the 860-acre Devils Hopyard State Park. The park, which includes camping and picnic facilities as well as miles of hiking trails, became a state park in 1919.

In centuries past, Abner Beebe established a sawmill and gristmill on opposite sides of the Eightmile River near the waterfall, and the tiny hamlet became known as Beebe's Mills. In 1774 Beebe's brother-in-law, John Chapman (whose name has become forever identified with Chapman Falls), acquired the property. The mills shut down in the mid-1890s.

The park's unusual name may have arisen from the numerous potholes that lie scattered about at the base of the falls. According to folklore, the potholes are the Devil's footprints as he hopped across the streambed. Another story suggests that the name came from a man named Dibble who

Chapman Falls—guaranteed to put on quite a show

grew hops in his garden for brewing beer. Over time, Dibble's Hopyard morphed into Devils Hopyard.

DIRECTIONS: From east of East Haddam (junction of CT 82 and CT 151) drive south on CT 82 east for less than 0.05 mile. Turn left onto Mt. Parnassus Road/Millington Road and proceed east for 5.9 miles, following signs for the Devils Hopyard State Park.

From south of Colchester, traveling on CT 11, get off at exit 5. Proceed west on Witch Hollow/Alexander/Salem Road for 2.5 miles (the last 1.0 mile being a dirt road). When you come to Haywardville Road, turn left and go 0.3 mile.

Coming from either direction, turn south from Haywardville Road onto Hopyard Road and go south for 0.7 mile. Then turn left onto Foxtown Road, go 70 feet, and immediately bear left into the parking area for Chapman Falls.

From the parking area walk straight across Foxtown Road to a kiosk that overlooks the top of the falls. Take the wide path to your right, which starts you heading down toward the bottom of the gorge. There are lateral views of the falls along the way. After a couple of hundred feet turn left and follow a side path which leads steeply down to a massive area of exposed bedrock facing the waterfall.

82

FALLS ON MUDDY BROOK

Location: Northeast of East Haddam (Middlesex County), Devils Hopyard State Park

Delorme Connecticut/Rhode Island Atlas and Gazetteer: p. 37, K13; **Estimated GPS:** 41°28.54'N; 72°20.53'W

Views: Head-on, lateral

Aesthetics: Fair/Good

Characteristics: Remote, scenic, small/medium-sized

Accessibility: 0.5-mile walk

Degree of Difficulty: Moderate

Information: Devils Hopyard State Park, 860-873-8566; trail map available at www.ct.gov/dep/lib /dep/stateparks/maps/devilshop yard.pdf

DESCRIPTION: These series of small falls (aka Mini Falls and Baby Falls), starting with a 15-foot high cascade, are formed on Muddy Brook—a small stream which rises from Will Cone Pond and flows into Eightmile River farther downstream.

The main cascade consists of a series of gentle, inclined drops totaling 15 feet in height.

DIRECTIONS: Follow the directions given in the previous entry for Chapman Falls. From the junction of Hopyard Road and Foxville Road by Chapman Falls, continue south on Hopyard Road for another 0.7 mile (or 1.4 miles from Haywardville Road). As soon as you cross over the third in a series of stone bridges on Hopyard Road, turn right into a small pull-out. If the space is occupied, park in one of several other pullouts in the vicinity.

Two small cascades are visible from the Hopyard Road bridge—a small waterslide downstream from the bridge and a small, 3-foot-high cascade just upstream.

Follow the red-blazed trail (an old road) upstream for 0.5 mile. Along the way, the road crosses Muddy Brook twice. At the first crossing you will see a small, 3-foot-high cascade upstream in the distance; at the second crossing you will pass directly by a 2-foot cascade on your right.

At 0.5 mile, turn right onto a white-blazed side path that takes you to the top of the main cascade in a couple of hundred feet. Cross over the footbridge and continue downhill on the white-blazed trail for 50 feet. Then bushwhack over to the base of the cascade, only 50 feet away.

FALLS ACCESSIBLE FROM I-84/I-384 AND US 6

I-84/US 6 crosses the Connecticut River from Hartford into eastern Connecticut west of Manchester. From here I-84 continues northeast until it enters Massachusetts north of Bigelow Hollow State Park; US 6 goes directly through the center of Manchester; and I-384 (an offshoot of I-84) skirts around the south side of Manchester.

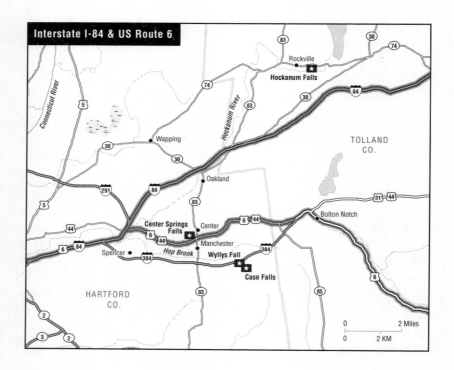

83

See page 220 for hiking map

WYLLYS FALLS

Location: Manchester (Hartford County)

Delorme Connecticut/Rhode Island Atlas and Gazetteer: p. 45, F18; **Estimated GPS:** 41°45.63'N; 72°29.69'W

Views: Head-on

Aesthetics: Excellent

Characteristics: Remote, scenic, large

Accessibility: 0.2-mile hike

Degree of Difficulty: Moderately difficult/bushwhack

Information: Manchester Land Conservation Trust, www .manchesterlandtrust.org

DESCRIPTION: Wyllys Falls, aka Bridal Veil Falls, is a 65-foot-high cascade on Birch Mountain Brook—a medium-sized stream which rises from the eastern slopes of Birch Mountain southeast of Manchester and flows into Porter Brook. The waterfall is in a deep gorge behind the old Case Brothers Mills on Glen Road, downstream from Case Falls (see next entry). Practically speaking, the gorge is so deep that the waterfall can only be reached by entering the gorge downstream and then hiking up to it.

Wyllys Falls, a short bushwhack leading into a box canyon

The ruins of a breached dam, which added another 20 feet to the height of the waterfall, can be seen at the top of the cascade—as well as the looming chimney that rises up from the old Case Brothers Mills further beyond.

HISTORY: Hayden Griswold, Jr., donated the land by the falls to the Manchester Land Conservation Trust in 1985.

The remains of an old copper mine are located a short distance downstream from the waterfall along the south bank. The mine operated briefly, and then stopped in 1905 when it became evident that the ore was too sparse and sporadic to justify any further mining efforts.

The waterfall is named after Ephraim Wyllys, an early property owner. The copper mine and a nearby street are also named after him.

DIRECTIONS: Driving east on I-384, get off at exit 3. Turn left onto CT 83 and drive south for 0.2 mile to Spring Street.

Driving west on I-384, get off at exit 3. Bear left onto Charter Oak Street (CT 534), and head west for 0.1 mile. Then turn left onto CT 83 and proceed south for 0.5 mile to Spring Street.

When you come to Spring Street turn left and proceed east for 1.3 miles. As soon as you pass by Tam Road on your right, pull over. Take note that you are in a residential area.

Directly across the street is a boulder with a memorial plaque. This is the entrance to land overseen by the Manchester Land Conservation Trust. Follow a clearly defined path that leads steeply downhill for several hundred feet to Birch Mountain Brook.

The trail essentially ends at this point, with no clearly defined path continuing to the falls (at least not at the time of this book's publication). Rock hop across Birch Mountain Brook and then follow the creek upstream along its flattened west bank for 0.2 mile. Be prepared for a short but somewhat demanding bushwhack due to blowdowns. Fortunately, getting lost should not be a problem since you have the stream to follow both up and back, and steep gorge walls to confine you to a narrow corridor. Just make a mental note of where your starting point is so that you don't go by it on the way back. The waterfall is at the rounded end of a box canyon.

84

CASE FALLS

Location: Manchester (Hartford County), Highland Park
Delorme Connecticut/Rhode Island Atlas and Gazetteer: p. 45, F18; **Estimated GPS:** 41°45.63'N; 72°29.39'W

Views: Head-on
Aesthetics: Good
Characteristics: Remote, medium-sized, partially dammed
Accessibility: Roadside
Degree of Difficulty: Easy

DESCRIPTION: Case Falls is a 25-foot-high dammed cascade on Birch Mountain Brook—a medium-sized stream which rises from the eastern slopes of Birch Mountain southeast of Manchester and flows into Porter Brook. Directly above the cascade is a stone bridge, which is now gated and closed off to the public. Part of the dam above the falls has been incorporated into it.

Native Americans called the falls *nip-pau, nip* being Native American for "water" and *pau* for "falls." These early Americans reportedly used several nearby springs for purposes of healing.

Case Falls—named after the Case brothers, Willard and Wells

HISTORY: During the 18th and 19th centuries, the falling waters of Birch Mountain Brook were used to power a number of industries.

The area is closely associated with A. Wells Case and A. Willard Case—twin brothers who set up a business to produce washed cotton in 1862, which they supplied to the Union Army during the Civil War. Later they erected a mill to produce album boards and a variety of other paper products. To help facilitate the business, the brothers also created machinery for papermaking, a blacksmith shop, and housing for their employees. Slowly the community grew into an area called Highland Park.

At one point the Case brothers planned to turn Highland Park into a spa, complete with hotels and cottages. When it became evident that this plan was never going to happen, they created a clear spring water and mineral water bottling plant in 1889 that became known as the Tonica Springs Company. The name Tonica—"tonic" with an *a* added on—was a subtle attempt to imply that the bottled waters had therapeutic powers.

The Case brothers proved to be civic-minded, making their land available to the public for hiking, ice skating, and picnicking. In 1903 A. Wells Case began constructing carriage roads, stone walls, and bridges. His son, Lawrence, completed the project in 1909.

DIRECTIONS: Driving east on I-384, get off at exit 3. Turn left onto CT 83 and drive south for 0.2 mile to Spring Street.

Driving west on I-384, get off at exit 3. Bear left onto Charter Oak Street (CT 534), and head west for 0.1 mile. Then turn left onto CT 83 and proceed south for 0.5 mile to Spring Street.

When you come to Spring Street turn left and proceed east for 1.6 miles. Pull over into a parking area on your right just before reaching a one-lane bridge.

Case Falls is upstream from the bridge, easily seen from either the road or by following a short path down to the streambed where more close-up views can be obtained.

85

〜

CENTER SPRINGS FALLS

Location: Manchester (Hartford County), Center Springs Park

Delorme Connecticut/Rhode Island Atlas and Gazetteer: p. 45, E14; **Estimated GPS:** 41°46.60'N; 72°31.30'W

Views: Lateral

Aesthetics: Fair

Characteristics: Urban, small, seasonal

Accessibility: 0.2-mile walk

Degree of Difficulty: Easy; descent to streambed—moderate

Information: Trail map available at http://recreation.townof manchester.org/documents/TrailMix Guide.pdf

Hours: 6 AM to 10 PM

DESCRIPTION: Center Springs Falls is on Bigelow Brook—a small stream which rises in Manchester and flows into the Hockanum River.

Two cascades can be seen where Bigelow Brook enters the east side of Center Springs Park. The uppermost waterfall is a 10-foot-high cascade where the stream issues from a culvert, dropping over an incline of black rocks onto the streambed below. It is difficult to tell how much of this waterfall is natural, and how much is artificial.

The second cascade, Center Springs Falls is an elongated 10-foot-high cascade, all natural, 100 feet downstream from the first waterfall. It is not as easily seen from above.

HISTORY: Center Springs Park, located in the heart of Manchester, contains 55 acres of land with a 6.1-acre pond. The pond was created in the 1920s. The park is named for its springs, the main one being near Center Street. From the 1920s through the mid-1970s the park was a popular site for skating and fishing.

Native Americans reportedly camped near Bigelow Brook and caught lamprey eels at the waterfall.

DIRECTIONS: Driving east on I-384, get off at exit 3. Turn right onto CT 83 and drive north for 1.0 mile.

Driving west on I-384, get off at exit 3. Bear left onto Charter Oak Street (CT 534), and go west for 0.1 mile. Then turn right onto CT 83 and drive north for 0.8 mile.

As soon as you reach the intersection with US 44/US 6 (Center Street), continue north (straight ahead) on CT 83 for another 100 feet. Then turn

Center Springs Falls, located in the heart of Manchester (ca. 1920 postcard)

left into Lincoln Center, where parking and pedestrian access to Center Springs Park is available.

From the parking area, walk down a long flight of stone stairs into the park and over toward the gorge. Then bear right, following a walkway that parallels the fenced-in south rim of the gorge. The walkway proceeds directly to the east end of the park, rounds the tip of the gorge, and then returns along the north rim of the gorge.

As soon as you go around the east end of the gorge, follow the walkway west along the north bank for over 100 feet. You will come to a 75-foot-long path on your left that leads down into the gorge. At this point you have traveled roughly 0.2 mile from the parking area.

As you descend into the ravine, the top of Center Springs Falls, to your right, will come into view for the first time. Once you know where the waterfall is, it is possible later to scamper around near the top of the ravine for better views.

Once down inside the ravine you will also get a better view of the upstream cascade, as well as the 30-foot-high cliffs that form the south wall of the gorge.

86

HOCKANUM FALLS

Location: Rockville (Tolland County)
Delorme Connecticut/Rhode Island Atlas and Gazetteer: p. 54, K7; **Estimated GPS:** 41°52.07'N; 72°26.63'W
Views: Head-on

Aesthetics: Fair/Good
Characteristics: Urban, historic, medium-sized
Accessibility: Roadside
Information: Rockville Downtown Association, 860-875-7439

DESCRIPTION: This 15-foot-high cascade is on the Hockanum River—a medium-sized river that rises from nearby Snipsic Lake (known locally as "The Snip") and flows into the Connecticut River southwest of East Hartford. Entering Rockville, the river moves underground through conduits, passing beneath streets and buildings unnoticed, until it reemerges at the falls.

HISTORY: The stone mill erected over the top of Hockanum Falls was originally called Dart's Stone Mill. Albert Dart built it in 1868, but unfortunately overextended himself financially after purchasing an enormous 55-foot diameter waterwheel to power three sections of the mill. When Dart died in 1882 Cyrus White took over the building, and the business became known as the White Manufacturing Company. Later, the name changed to the J. J. Regan Company. Today the stone mill is home to Amberbelle Textiles, a producer of fabrics.

During precolonial days, Snipsic Lake was a favorite campground for Native Americans. At that time the lake was only half its present size.

Through a Preservation of the Place Project Grant funded by the Connecticut Main Street Center, along with help from the Hockanum River Linear Park Committee, TO Design, the Vernon Public Works Department, the Connecticut Valley Fence Company, citizens, and property owners Howard Fromson and Barbara and Sol Cantor, historic plaques have been erected at key spots along the river to narrate the Hokanum River's industrial past.

DIRECTIONS: From I-84, get off at exit 67. Proceed north on CT 31 for approximately 1.2 miles. Then turn left onto CT 74 and head downhill for less than 0.1 mile. Pull into a parking area on your left from where excellent views of the falls can be obtained.

Just downstream is a 30-foot-high dam and stonework opposite Ano-coil, maker of plate products.

An old factory spans the top of Hockanum Falls.

FALLS ACCESSIBLE FROM CT 32

CT 32 enters Connecticut from Massachusetts, passes by Shenipsit State Forest, and then proceeds directly south, paralleling the Willimantic River once it reaches Stafford Springs. At Willimantic, CT 32 briefly changes its allegiance to the Shetucket River, which it follows until Williams Crossing. The route finally reaches its terminus at Yantic.

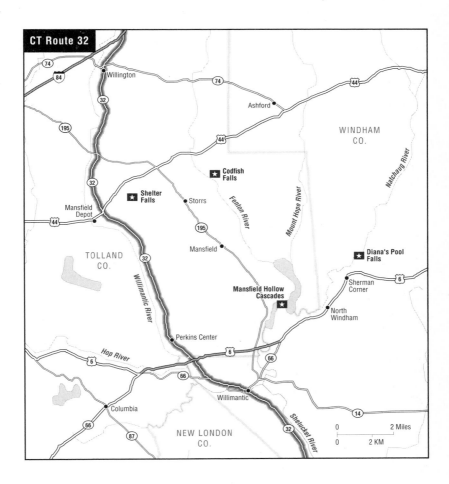

87

CODFISH FALLS

Location: East of Mansfield Four
Corners (Tolland County)
**Delorme Connecticut/Rhode
Island Atlas and Gazetteer:**
p. 46, B8; **Estimated GPS:**
41°49.47'N; 72°13.59'W
Views: Head-on, lateral

Aesthetics: Good
Characteristics: Remote, historic,
scenic, medium-sized
Accessibility: Several hundred-
foot walk
Degree of Difficulty: To top—
easy; to bottom—moderate

DESCRIPTION: Codfish Falls is a 15-foot-high, three-tier waterfall on Fishers Brook—a small stream which rises from hills further north and flows into the Fenton River, 0.3 mile downstream from the falls. A 3-foot cascade is just downstream from the main falls.

DIRECTIONS: From Mansfield Depot (junction of US 44 and CT 32) take US 44 (Middle Turnpike) northeast for 2.6 miles to Mansfield Four Corners (junction of US 44 and CT 195). From here continue east on US 44 for another 1.7 miles. When you come to Codfish Falls Road, turn right

A good dose of Codfish Falls

and head southeast for nearly 1.0 mile. Turn into a tiny, drivewaylike pull-out on your right immediately after crossing Fishers Brook.

Walk downstream for several hundred feet along the south bank, following an old sluiceway where water presumably once tumbled down from the dammed pond east of Codfish Falls Road to a mill below the waterfall. The trail leads to the top of Codfish Falls. From here, a short, steep path leads down to the bottom of the falls should you want a closer look.

88

SHELTER FALLS

Location: Southwest of Mansfield Four Corners (Tolland County), Mansfield Shelter Falls Park
Delorme Connecticut/Rhode Island Atlas and Gazetteer: p. 46, C4; **Estimated GPS:** 41°48.74'N; 72°17.20'W
Views: Head-on, lateral
Aesthetics: Fair

Characteristics: Remote, small, rock shelter main attraction
Accessibility: 0.1-mile walk
Degree of Difficulty: Moderately easy
Information: Trail map available at www.mansfieldct.gov/filestorage /1904/5357/shelter_falls.pdf

DESCRIPTION: Shelter Falls, consisting of several drops totaling 3–4 feet, is on Cedar Swamp Brook—a small stream which rises near Mansfield Four Corners. The falls' name arose from a rock shelter adjacent to the stream, where an inclined slab of bedrock extends for 30 feet.

HISTORY: Mansfield Shelter Falls Park, a 75-acre wooded tract of land, contains 1.7 miles of trails. Old mill ruins are located at the junction of Cedar Swamp Brook and Nelson Brook (a small tributary), 0.1 mile downstream from the road. The town of Mansfield oversees the park.

DIRECTIONS: From Mansfield Depot (junction of US 44 and CT 32) take US 44 northeast for 0.7 mile. Turn right onto Bone Mill Road and proceed southeast for 0.4 mile. Then turn left onto Birch Road and head northeast for 0.2–0.3 mile. Look for the Shelter Falls sign, blue with gold letters, on your right. There is a sizeable parking area on your left just before the sign.

Follow the wide, white-blazed trail southeast for 0.1 mile, initially paralleling Nelson Brook, and then veering left to follow Cedar Swamp Brook.

As soon as you walk over a footbridge spanning Cedar Swamp Brook, turn left and follow the white-blazed trail upstream for 100 feet to the shelter cave and cascades.

If you wish, you can continue to the top of the rock shelter and then follow the white-blazed trail as it loops back to the footbridge.

This is one hike where you will undoubtedly find the rock shelter to be of more interest than the cascades.

89

DIANA'S POOL FALLS

Location: South Chaplin (Windham County)
Delorme Connecticut/Rhode Island Atlas and Gazetteer: p. 47, E14; **Estimated GPS:** 41°46.69'N; 72°07.85'W
Views: Head-on, lateral
Aesthetics: Good

Characteristics: Remote, scenic, small
Accessibility: Lower cascade—several hundred foot walk; Diana's Pool Falls—0.05-mile walk
Degree of Difficulty: Moderately easy

DESCRIPTION: Diana's Pool Falls, aka Cow Sluice Rapids, is one of a series of small falls on the Natchaug River—a medium-sized stream which rises near Eastford, and joins with the Willimantic River at Willimantic, to create the Shetucket River. None of the cascades are much higher than 3 feet, but they are sizeable enough to furnish white-water paddlers with Class II–IV thrills. A highly popular site during the summer, expect crowds on a nice day—though no swimming is allowed.

Diana's Pool Falls drops 3–4 feet through a narrow slot into an enormous pool of water called Diana's Pool. A rocky amphitheater with huge slabs of bedrock and boulders surrounds the pool. A shelter cave lies directly under the enormous inclined section of bedrock facing the falls.

Encountered farther downstream, near Diana's Pool Bridge, is a short but very impressive gorge where the river drops over a small cascade. Once again there is much exposed bedrock, with large boulders in proliferation. Two long cavities can be seen along the west wall of the gorge; the higher one being 30 feet long, and the lower one 10 feet.

Diana's Pool Falls—as lovely as a goddess

HISTORY: Possibly Diana's Pool was named after Diana, the goddess of the hunt, moon, and birthing in Roman mythology.

A short distance downstream from the falls, near the parking area, is Diana's Pool Bridge, a 75-foot-long, concrete arch structure built in 1926.

The name of the river, *natchaug,* is Nipmuck for "between rivers."

Chaplin is named after its first settler, Benjamin Chaplin, a businessman who made baskets and trays.

DIRECTIONS: From northeast of Willimantic (junction of US 6 and CT 66), drive northeast on US 6 for 3.7 miles to Sherman Corners. Turn left onto CT 198 and head north for 0.5 mile. Then turn right onto Diana's Pool Road just before crossing over the Natchaug River and, after 50 feet, turn left into the parking area for Diana's Pool. Follow the fishing access site path north.

To first cascade: After 100 feet, follow a path to your left which leads immediately to a spectacular gorge with a small cascade at its mouth.

To Diana's Pool Falls: Continue north on the main trail for 0.05 mile to an enormous inclined slab of bedrock which faces Diana's Pool Falls.

If you wish, you can follow the path further along the east bank up to the top of Diana's Pool Falls, but there is little to be gained by doing so, for the best views are those that face the falls head-on.

90
MANSFIELD HOLLOW CASCADES

Location: Mansfield Center (Tolland County), Mansfield Hollow Historic District
Delorme Connecticut/Rhode Island Atlas and Gazetteer: p. 46, F11; **Estimated GPS:** 41°45.59'N; 72°10.84'W
Views: Lateral

Aesthetics: Good
Characteristics: Urban, historic, scenic, small, partially dammed
Accessibility: 200-foot walk
Degree of Difficulty: Easy
Information: Trail map available at www.ct.gov/dep/lib/dep/state parks/maps/mansfieldhollow.pdf

DESCRIPTION: A number of small cascades and rapids are below the Mansfield Hollow Dam on the Natchaug River—a medium-sized stream which rises near Eastford and joins with the Willimantic River at Willimantic to form the Shetucket River.

The uppermost cascade is 8 feet high and part of a horseshoe-shaped dam that spans the river a mere 100 feet downriver from the massive, towering Mansfield Hollow Dam. Here the river compresses, entering a small gorge where a number of small cascades can be seen within the span of 100 feet. The last cascade drops 3 feet over a diagonal shelf in the bedrock.

HISTORY: The U.S. Army Corps of Engineers created Mansfield Hollow Lake, a 500-acre reservoir, in the early 1950s for flood control. The impoundment inundated Turnip Meadows, a swampy area at the confluence of the Fenton, Mount Hope, and Natchaug Rivers.

The cascades are located in the 18-acre historic district of Mansfield Hollow, whose 17 buildings were placed on the National Register of Historic Places in 1979.

The enormous, two-story high, 155-foot-long stone building near the cascades—the centerpiece of Mansfield Hollow—is called Kirby's Mill, named after the George Kirby who bought the mill in 1902. The National Thread Company originally built the mill in 1882, but SEA (Science Engineering Associates, Inc.) occupies it presently.

DIRECTIONS: From north of Willimantic (junction of US 6 and CT 195), drive north on CT 195 for roughly 1.5 miles. Turn right onto Mansfield Hollow Road and proceed northeast for 0.5 mile. Then turn right onto Mansfield Hollow Extension and continue east for another 0.1 mile until you reach the parking area at the Mansfield Hollow Dam.

Walk back down Mansfield Hollow Extension for 100 feet and turn left, passing through an opening in the guardrail. Proceed directly across the field to reach the river, some 150 feet away. Then walk over to the mouth of the gorge, where large stone blocks on the north bank are visible proof of times of past industrialization. It is possible to scamper down onto the bedrock next to the river here.

The lowermost cascades are found 100 feet farther downstream.

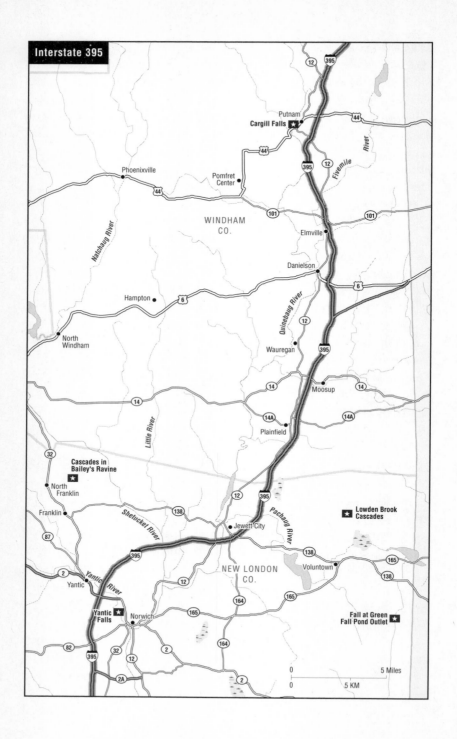

Interstate 395

FALLS ACCESSIBLE FROM I-395

I-395 (Governor John Davis Lodge Turnpike) enters the northeast corner of the state from Webster, Massachusetts, and follows close to the border with Rhode Island past Putnam and several small towns. After skirting by Plainfield, I-395 turns southwest, skipping past Norwich, to parallel the Thames River. It eventually reaches I-95, west of New London.

91

CARGILL FALLS

Location: Putnam (Windham County)
Delorme Connecticut/Rhode Island Atlas and Gazetteer: p. 57, 115; **Estimated GPS:** 41°55.07'N; 71°54.60'W
Views: Head-on, lateral
Aesthetics: Good
Characteristics: Urban, historic, small, broad

Accessibility: 0.1-mile walk
Degree of Difficulty: Easy
Information: Trail map available at www.putnamct.us/putnamat glance/River%20Mills%20Heritage %20Trail/River%20Mills%20Heritage %20Trail.htm

DESCRIPTION: Cargill Falls, aka, the Great Falls of the Quinebaug River, consist of a series of small cascades and rapids on the Quinebaug River—a large river which rises west of Southbridge, Massachusetts, and flows into the Thames River at Norwich. The falls are located directly below a broad dam which, except for being intercepted by a sizeable island near the center of the river, spans the entire width of the Quinebaug. The island divides the river into two main channels, including several secondary channels that run over the island like rivulets. All of these channels contain an assortment of tiny cascades. The river momentarily turns into one giant kaleidoscope of broken streams, rivulets, and cascades.

Just below the falls, connecting Putnam with Pomfret, is the Pomfret Bridge, from where clear views of the river and cascades can be obtained.

HISTORY: Prior to 1720, David Howe established Cargill Falls' first industry. In 1730 a Scotsman named Captain Benjamin Cargill purchased Howe's property and built a new mill. His gristmill was able to grind out

Cargill Falls once supported a huge number of industries.

five hundred bushels of corn daily using three large millstones which Cargill had installed.

In 1760 a distillery, malt house, fulling mill, trip-hammer shop, sawmill, blacksmith shop, and churning mill (Pomfret's first creamery) were added.

In 1807 the Pomfret Manufacturing Company started the Pomfret Cotton Mills to produce textile products. It is the oldest site of its kind in the nation. Additional components were added over the years, and the site later became known as Cargill Falls Mill.

Putnam was originally called Aspinock, a name which later changed to Putnam to honor General Israel Putnam, a Revolutionary War soldier. After the great flood of 1955 severely damaged the town, Putnam was literally reborn. Putnam Green Power presently utilizes the waterfall to generate hydroelectric power.

DIRECTIONS: From I-395 get off at exit 96 and drive west on CT 12 for 1.0 mile. Turn left onto US 44 and head south for 0.2 mile. Just before crossing over the Pomfret Bridge, turn right onto Kennedy Drive and proceed west for 0.1 mile. Then turn left into a municipal parking area next to Rotary Park.

Proceeding on foot, follow the paved River Walk Trail east as it parallels the Quinebaug River. In 0.1 mile you will approach the Pomfret Bridge, from where excellent views of the cascades and gorge can be obtained (views can also be had from the River Walk Trail paralleling Kennedy Drive).

92

CASCADES IN BAILEY'S RAVINE

Location: East of North Franklin (New London County)
Delorme Connecticut/Rhode Island Atlas and Gazetteer: p. 38, B1; **Estimated GPS:** 41°38.00'N; 72°08.27'W
Views: Head-on, lateral

Aesthetics: Excellent
Characteristics: Remote, scenic, medium-sized, awesome gorge
Accessibility: To gorge—0.8-mile hike; through gorge—0.4-mile hike
Degree of Difficulty: Moderately difficult

DESCRIPTION: Bailey's Falls, aka Ayer's Falls, consists of a series of cascades formed in Bailey's Ravine on Bailey's Brook—a small tributary to Beaver Brook that rises between Avery Hill and Pleasure Hill.

The deeply set ravine extends in a north/south orientation for 0.4 mile. The most prominent waterfalls in the ravine are the 10-foot-high cascade at the mouth of Bailey's Ravine and the two 6-foot-high cascades at the ravine's terminus. One of the waterfalls historically has been called the Water Nymph.

Just as impressive as the waterfalls, however, is Bailey's Ravine itself, whose immensity has to be seen to be truly appreciated. In many places the ravine is chasmlike, with walls rising up steeply to form narrow passageways. Everywhere you look, you will see the deep greens of moss commingling with the dusky gray-green colors of the bedrock and the giant rocks that litter the landscape. The ravine is formed out of Scotland schist, a metamorphic rock.

HISTORY: In 1989, Helena E. Bailey-Spencer, wife of former Lieutenant Governor Samuel R. Spencer, willed Bailey's Ravine (an 80-acre natural area) to the Nature Conservancy; the site is dedicated to her.

Ayer's Gap and Ayer's Falls are named after John Ayer Trapper, the first settler in the town of Franklin, who lived there as early as 1665.

In earlier times the ravine was a major attraction on a trolley line that ran through Ayer's Gap from Willimantic.

DIRECTIONS: From I-395 get off at exit 83 and head northwest on CT 97 for roughly 3.2 miles to the village of Baltic. Turn left onto CT 207 and head west for 3.4 miles. Pull into a paved parking area on your right immediately after passing by the second turn for Ayer Road.

Waterfalls have formed at both ends of Bailey's Ravine.

Approaching from North Franklin (junction of CT 32 and CT 207), drive east on CT 207 (Pond Road) for 1.4 miles. Pull into a paved parking area on your left where a sign states BAILEY'S RAVINE AT AYER'S GAP, virtually opposite Under the Mountain Road.

From the east end of the parking area, follow the white-blazed trail uphill through a steep rock gully. The trail leads to an overlook and then goes around the east side of Avery Hill. At roughly 0.8 mile the trail crosses the head of Bailey's Ravine (41°38.45'N; 72°08.18'W), where a scenic 10-foot-high cascade can be seen to your right.

From here, leave the white-blazed trail behind to hike downstream through Bailey's Ravine. At times you will be traveling inside the gorge; at other times along its banks and walls. Trails along both sides of the gorge ensure that you can switch from one side to the other when the way ahead seemingly becomes impassable.

The ravine finally ends at Ayer Road, 0.1 mile north of CT 207.

93

YANTIC FALLS

Location: Norwich (New London County), Yantic Falls Historic District
Delorme Connecticut/Rhode Island Atlas and Gazetteer: p. 38, G/H4; **Estimated GPS:** 41°32.04'N; 72°05.33'W

Views: Head-on, lateral
Aesthetics: Excellent
Characteristics: Urban, historic, large
Accessibility: 0.05-mile walk
Degree of Difficulty: Easy

DESCRIPTION: Yantic Falls (aka Norwich Falls, Indian Leap Falls, and Uncas Leap Falls) is a dammed, 40-foot-high cascade on the Yantic River—a medium-sized river which rises from Savin Lake and joins with the Quinebaug River in Norwich to form the Thames River.

Just upstream from the falls, a pedestrian bridge erected in 1904 by the Berlin Bridge Company spans the river, providing wonderful views into the interior of the gorge where the river compresses momentarily before being released. Crossing the river diagonally next to the footbridge is a railroad truss bridge built by the Central Vermont Railroad that is still in use.

Yantic Falls in front of a stupendous gorge

HISTORY: Long before the arrival of Europeans, Yantic Falls was a favored encampment of the Mohegans. In 1643 a decisive battle took place in which the Mohegans, led by their sachem, Uncas, resoundingly defeated the Narragansetts, a rival tribe. According to folklore, many of the Narragansetts died trying to leap across the gorge to escape. Considering the width of the Yantic River, it would have taken a superhuman jump to make it to the other side. Undoubtedly, those Narragansetts who toppled into the chasm were either pushed by the vengeful Mohegans or simply took their chances jumping onto the rocks and water below.

Since the 1600s the falls has served many industrial purposes, from powering John Elderkin's gristmill in the 1600s to a nail factory in 1813; from a paper mill in 1818 to a cotton mill and woolen mill in 1826. Activities by the falls continued right into the early 1900s. Today two large mills along the east bank have been converted into housing units.

The word *yantic* is possibly Mohegan for "extended river," "as far as the tidal stream," or "on this side of the stream."

The Yantic Falls Historic District contains 11 buildings whose names were added onto the National Register of Historic Places in 1972.

Improvements at the small waterfall park were made possible through a

State of Connecticut grant, the Department of Environmental Protection (now the Department of Energy and Environmental Protection), and funding through the city of Norwich.

The rock formation known as Indian Leap is a 150-foot-high precipice along the west bank, roughly 100 feet downstream from the falls.

DIRECTIONS: From I-395, going south, get off at exit 81; going north, get off at exit 81A.

Head east on CT 2 for about 1.1 miles to where CT 169 comes in on the left. Continue on CT 2 (Washington Street), now bearing south, for another 0.7 mile. Turn right onto Sacham Street and proceed west for 0.3 mile. Then turn left onto Yantic Street and go 0.1 mile. Park either in a large, unmarked parking area to your right just past the falls (next to warehouse number three) or along the street.

From the parking lot, walk northwest for 100 feet to reach the north end of the Yantic Falls dam, where excellent lateral views of the falls can be obtained.

Next walk up to the kiosk and proceed across the footbridge spanning the Yantic River for views looking downriver into the interior of the gorge. At the west end of the footbridge, continue south along the railed walkway for another 50 feet. Once again you will be afforded excellent lateral views of the falls. At the point where a high footbridge crosses over the railroad tracks, informal paths on the left lead off to head-on views of Yantic Falls.

94

LOWDEN BROOK CASCADES

Location: North of Voluntown (New London County)
Delorme Connecticut/Rhode Island Atlas and Gazetteer: p. 39, C18; **Estimated GPS:** 41°36.32'N; 71°51.63'W
Views: Lateral
Aesthetics: Fair/Good
Characteristics: Remote, scenic, small

Accessibility: 0.4-mile hike
Degree of Difficulty: Moderate due to footing
Information: Trail map available in Ann T. Colson (ed.), *Connecticut Walk Book: The Guide to the Blue-Blazed Hiking Trails of Eastern Connecticut* (19th ed.), (Connecticut Forest & Park Association, 2006), page 237.

DESCRIPTION: These series of cascades are formed on Lowden Brook—a small stream which rises northeast of Bare Hill and flows into Mount Misery Brook further downstream.

The lowermost cascade is 3 feet high where the stream drops over a section of raised bedrock and boulders. Less than 100 feet further upstream is the main cascade, where a diagonal shelf of bedrock pushes the stream partially to one side and then down a short flume past two large boulders into a tiny pool. It is a drop of roughly 5 feet. Two additional small cascades are seen above the main one.

HISTORY: Voluntown's name goes back to when the area was set aside for "volunteers" of King Philip's War. Gradually "Volunteer Town" morphed into Voluntown.

The Pachaug Trail begins at the northern end of Pachaug Pond and ends at Green Fall Pond. The hike in this chapter follows only a tiny portion of the 30-mile-long trail.

DIRECTIONS: From I-395 get off at exit 85. Head east on CT 138 (Voluntown Road) for 6.5 miles to the junction of CT 138 and CT 49, east of Voluntown. Turn left onto CT 49 and drive north for 2.5 miles. When you come to Stone Hill Road turn left and drive west for 0.9 mile to the Lowden Brook Picnic Area, which is on your left just after you bear right at a fork in the road.

To reach the cascades, follow the blue-blazed Pachaug Trail north for 0.4 mile, paralleling the east bank of Lowden Brook as you head upstream. Be prepared for mud, rocks, and roots across sections of the trail.

ADDITIONAL CASCADE: A waterfall incorporated into a large stone dam can be seen at the outlet at Green Fall Pond.

From east of Voluntown (junction of CT 49 and CT 138), continue southeast on CT 138 for another 2.1 miles. Turn right onto Green Fall Road and proceed south for 2.4 miles to a small pullout on your left. Follow the blue-blazed loop trail opposite the pullout for over 0.6 mile to reach the outlet dam.

Maps Addendum

Bunnell's Falls, Hartford County

JACK'S BROOK CASCADE (ROXBURY) *(page 46)*

NONNEWAUG FALLS (BETHLEHEM) *(page 74)*

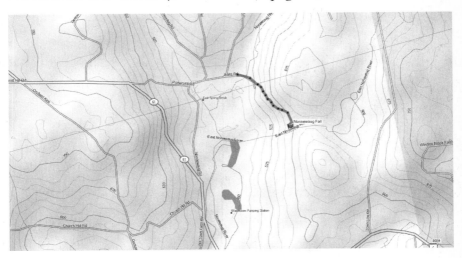

SPRUCE BROOK FALLS (BEACON FALLS) *(page 79)*

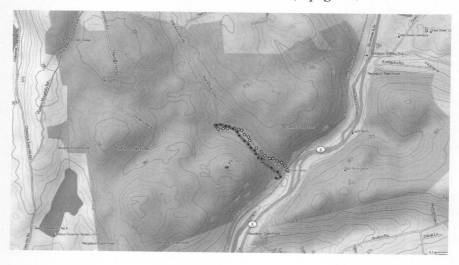

PRYDDEN BROOK FALLS (STEVENSON) *(page 92)*

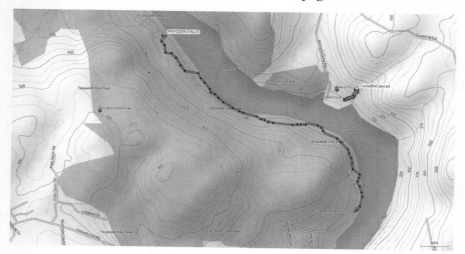

FARMILL RIVER FALLS (SHELTON) *(page 94)*

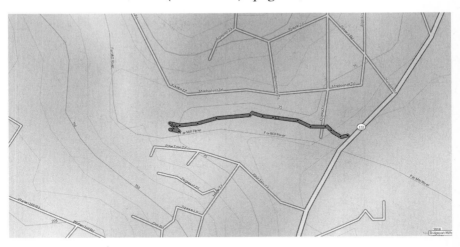

WHITE HILLS BROOK CASCADES (SHELTON) *(page 98)*

FALLS ON FALLS BROOK (WEST HARTLAND) *(page 103)*

CASCADES ALONG WESTLEDGE TRAIL
(WEST GRANBY AND WEST SIMSBURY) *(page 111)*

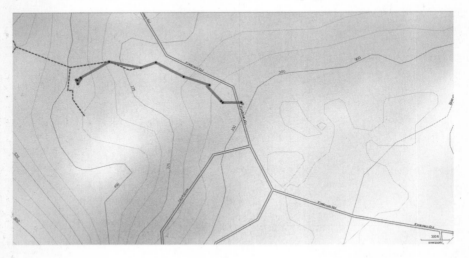

WATERFALL ON CATHLES TRAIL (SIMSBURY) *(page 116)*

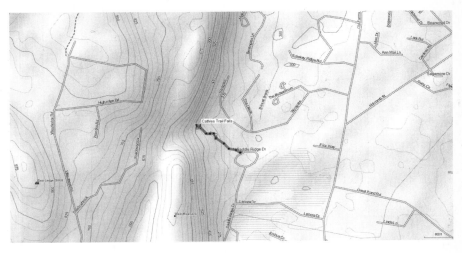

SESSIONS WOODS FALLS (BURLINGTON) *(page 121)*

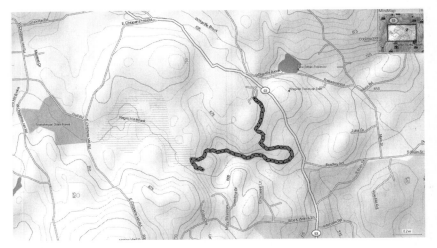

ROARING BROOK FALLS (CHESHIRE) *(page 124)*

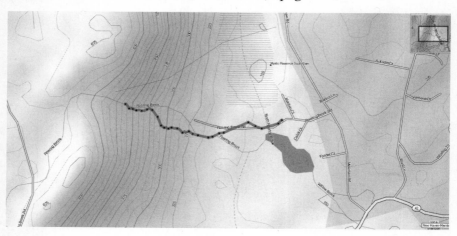

SPRUCE GLEN FALLS (WALLINGFORD) *(page 142)*

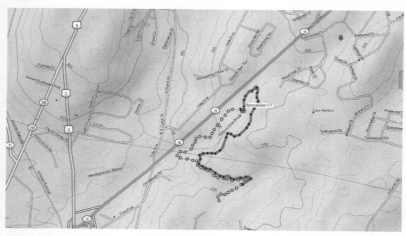

STAIR BROOK FALLS (DURHAM) *(page 145)*

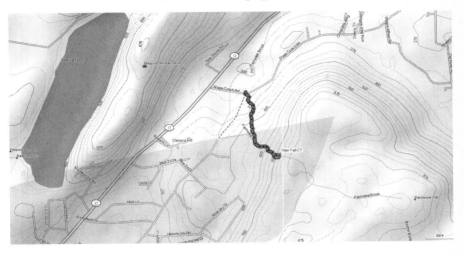

FLAT BROOK FALLS (EAST GLASTONBURY) *(page 164)*

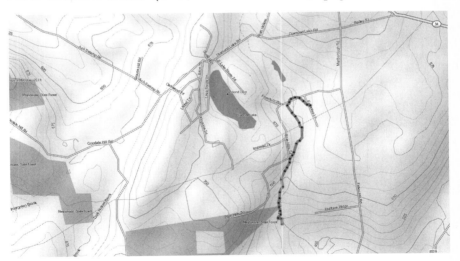

CRYSTAL CASCADE (PORTLAND) *(page 166)*

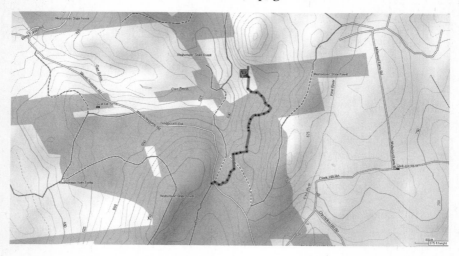

DAY POND BROOK FALLS (NORTH WESTCHESTER) *(page 171)*

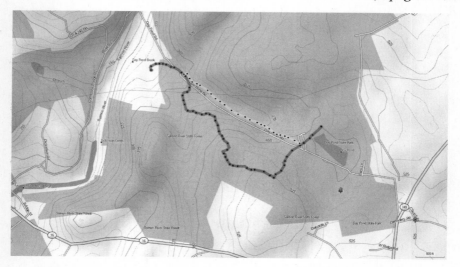

GLEN FALLS (COBALT) *(page 176)*

WATERFALL AT SHEEPSKIN HOLLOW PRESERVE (EAST HADDAM) *(page 179)*

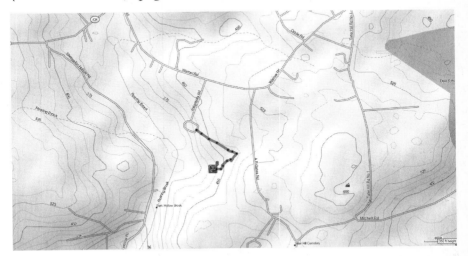

WYLLYS FALLS (MANCHESTER) *(page 185)*

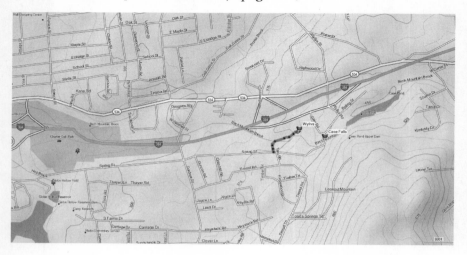

Additional Resources

Still River Gorge, Robertsville, Litchfield County

BOOKS:

Joseph Bushee Jr., *Waterfalls of Connecticut* (N.P.: Joseph Bushee Jr., 2011), e-book.

Greg Parsons & Kate B. Watson, *New England Waterfalls: A Guide to More than 400 Cascades and Waterfalls* (Woodstock, VT: Countryman Press, 2010).

WATERFALL WEBSITES:

www.ctwaterfalls.com: Website by David A. Ellis, Connecticut's premier waterfall expert and organizer of the Connecticut waterfall database

www.geology.com/waterfalls: Listing of locations and GPS coordinates

www.newenglandwaterfalls.com/connecticut.php: Website based on book by Greg Parsons and Kate B. Watson

www.northeastwaterfalls.com: A catalog by Dean Goss of waterfalls in the northeastern United States, including many postcard images and photos

www.rvsee.wikidot.com/ct-waterfalls: A listing of prominent Connecticut waterfalls

www.swimmingholes.org/ct.html: A statewide listing of swimming holes, some of which are associated with waterfalls

WATERFALL PHOTOGRAPHERS (CONNECTICUT):

Tim Barnes: www.naturephotojournal.com

Christy and Jan Butler: www.berkshirephotos.com

Justin Coleman: www.trailsoffreedom.com/connecticuts-best-waterfalls

Michael Farslow: www.farslowfotos.smugmug.com/Landscapes/waterfalls -of-Connecticut/

New Haven Camera Club: http://newhavencameraclub.blogspot.com

Christopher Rees: www.christopherrees.com/photos/v/outdoors/ct_waterfalls

Vincent Sapone: www.vincentsapone.com/ctwaterfalls/ctwaterfalls.html

HIKING GROUPS:

Appalachian Mountain Club, Connecticut Chapter: www.ct-amc.org

Barefoot Hikers of Connecticut (Wallingford): www.meetup.com/ct -barefooters

Meshomasic Hiking Club (Cobalt): www.meshomasichikingclub.org

Green Mountain Club, Connecticut Section: www.conngmc.com

Hartford Area Hiking Meetup Group: www.meetup.com/Hartford-Area -Hiking

New Haven Hiking Club: www.nhhc.info/schedule.htm

Salmon Brook Hiking Club (Granby): www.granbyhikers.tripod.com/frames
Hiking Group for Singles and Friends (Connecticut/New York): www.the
hikinggroup.com

HIKING WEBSITES THAT INCLUDE WATERFALLS:

www.ctmuseumquest.com: Website by Stephen Wood, an explorer and
writer whose focus is on areas of interest in Connecticut

ORGANIZATIONS:

Appalachian Trail Conservancy: www.appalachiantrail.org
Connecticut Bureau of Outdoor Recreation, State Parks Division; 860-
424-3200
Connecticut Department of Energy and Environmental Protection: www
.ct.gov/dep
Connecticut Forest and Park Association; 860-346-2372: www.ctwood
lands.org
Friends of Connecticut State Parks, Inc.: www.friendsctstateparks.org
The Nature Conservancy, Connecticut Chapter: www.nature.org/our
initiatives/regions/northamerica/unitedstates/connecticut/index.htm